Manifesting the Glory

How to Carry God's Presence and Power in Everyday Life

Dameyan Cole

Title: *Manifesting the Glory: How to Carry God's Presence and Power in Everyday Life*

Author: Dameyan Cole

ISBN: 9798292272366

Printed in: United States of America

Edition: First Edition

Disclaimer

This book is a work of Christian nonfiction written for personal growth, reflection, and spiritual development. The insights and interpretations expressed are those of the author and do not necessarily represent the views of any denomination, church body, or organization. While every effort has been made to ensure the accuracy of biblical references, historical context, and theological interpretation, the author and publisher assume no responsibility for any errors or for the results obtained from the application of the material contained herein. Readers are encouraged to seek biblical counsel and the guidance of the Holy Spirit in all areas of faith and practice.

For permissions, please contact:

✉@ orlandocolebooks@gmail.com

Dedication

To every seeker of His presence—those who have dared to leave behind routine comfort and pursue the throne room of heaven—I dedicate this book to you. You who have wrestled through prayer in the night, fasted not to be seen but to be filled, given sacrificially in seasons of doubt, and worshipped in hidden rooms when no one watched. May these pages meet you in your quiet longing and fan the fire of expectation in your soul.

To the mothers and fathers, the teachers and laborers, the missionaries, pastors, intercessors, and students—ordinary vessels poised by love—to carry the extraordinary weight of His glory. You may never stand on stage or trend on social media. Yet your lives are altars; your prayers, incense. May God honor your hidden obedience with visible presence.

To those in pain, those in waiting, to the broken who have not stopped hoping—may this book call you beyond coping to communion, beyond comfort to calling. You are not overlooked. Your altar is not empty. The same God who parted seas cares about what lies within you. May His presence flood your wounded places with resurrection power.

And to every reader who holds this book—whether you are burning or battered—may these chapters be more than words. May they be flint to your heart, stirring a fire that refuses to die. May the disciplines of prayer, fasting, worship, generosity, obedience, and cruciform living become not burdens, but breaths of the Spirit. And may the overflow of His presence not just visit your moments—but dwell in your life.

This is not merely a book. It is an invitation: to be hidden, to be broken, to be fired up... so that through you, Heaven can be seen. May you walk each step not just towards glory—but as glory, captivating the world by the radiance of the One who lives in you.

Table of Contents

Introduction: The Hunger for Glory

There is a deep cry rising across the earth. It echoes through sanctuaries, whispers in boardrooms, trembles in the halls of governments, and groans in the silence of midnight intercessors. It is the sound of people yearning for more— more of God, more of His power, more of His tangible presence in everyday life. This is not a cry for religion, performance, or comfort. It is a hunger for glory.

For too long, believers have settled for a version of Christianity that feels powerless, domesticated, and ordinary. Church services are attended, songs are sung, and prayers are spoken, but the question remains in many hearts: Where is the God of glory? Where is the weighty presence that parted seas, shattered prison doors, and raised the dead? Where is the nearness that made prophets tremble and demons flee? Where is the abiding presence that causes lives to transform, atmospheres to shift, and nations to bow?

This book was not born out of curiosity. It was born out of necessity. It is a divine interruption—a prophetic summons for every believer who dares to believe that the glory of God is not reserved for a chosen few or distant revivalists. It is for the teacher in the classroom, the nurse in the hospital, the pastor in the pulpit, and the mother in the kitchen. It is for those who burn with a holy dissatisfaction and refuse to accept a life absent of divine presence.

The glory of God is not an abstract doctrine. It is not an occasional cloud that descends during a worship set. It is the very essence of who God is—His nature revealed, His power unveiled, His beauty displayed. When Moses cried, "Show me Your glory," he was not asking for a thrill; he was pleading for the nearness of God to become visible, tangible, and transforming. And that same cry still ascends from the earth today (Exodus 33:18).

God's glory is not a moment to be visited—it is a realm to be inhabited. It is not for the spiritually elite—it is for the spiritually hungry. And while glory is sovereign, it does not rest arbitrarily. God entrusts His glory to those who are willing to be set apart, who choose death to self, who embrace the disciplines of the Spirit, and who walk in deep reverence. Glory cannot be manufactured. It can only be manifested through yielded vessels who understand what it costs and why it matters.

This book is a journey through that cost. It is an invitation into a lifestyle that births glory on earth. Each chapter is a doorway, opening into truths that many have lost, misunderstood, or ignored. These are not theories or opinions. They are spiritual laws, drawn from the Word of God and verified through real testimonies, historical awakenings, and the unwavering reliability of Scripture.

The road to manifesting the glory is not glamorous. It begins with crucifixion. The flesh must die so the Spirit can reign. There is no shortcut. Jesus Himself, though fully divine, demonstrated this path. He fasted, prayed, obeyed, and surrendered. He modeled the disciplines not because He needed them, but because we would. He showed us how to walk in glory while still wrapped in flesh. And now, He calls us to do the same.

Fasting is not a diet—it is a declaration of dependence. Prayer is not a performance—it is communion with the King. Giving is not a transaction—it is a breaking of the grip of greed so that heaven's resources can flow through our hands. Holiness is not legalism—it is the clothing of those who walk closely with God. Worship is not a musical style—it is a posture of heart that says, "You are worthy, even when I am weary." And obedience is not optional—it is the bridge between revelation and manifestation.

Many have mistaken busyness for fruitfulness and charisma for anointing. But the glory exposes what man cannot see. It reveals whether we are truly carrying God or merely performing for applause. This is why many avoid it. Glory demands death before it reveals life. But oh, what life it brings. When the glory comes, sickness bows, strongholds break, families heal, and nations tremble. When the glory rests upon a life, it speaks louder than sermons and lasts longer than events. It makes ordinary people walk in extraordinary power without ever needing the spotlight.

There is a generation rising that will not be satisfied with borrowed fire. They will not live off the testimonies of others. They want to see God for themselves. They want to walk into rooms and see atmospheres shift, not because they are impressive, but because they are surrendered. They long to be burning bushes—ordinary things set ablaze by an extraordinary God. They will not be content with emotional highs; they want sustained habitation.

This generation will be marked by discipline, not just desire. They will be people of secret history—those who have wrestled in prayer when no one saw, fasted when no one knew, and given when it hurt. They will be misjudged, misunderstood, and mislabeled, but they will carry something that cannot be denied: glory. It will rest on their words, their presence, and their lives.

This book is not written to entertain or impress. It is a call to die so you can truly live. It will confront the areas of compromise and ca you into a higher way. It will awaken the desire for more of God and give you the tools to host Him well. It will not always be comfortable, but it will always be worth it.

Throughout the pages that follow, you will be challenged to examine your habits, renew your mind, and embrace disciplines that have been forgotten by a distracted church. You will learn how to cultivate a lifestyle where the glory is not occasional, but continual. You will discover that fasting is not punishment—it is preparation. You will understand that giving is not loss—it is unlocking supernatural supply. You will begin to see prayer not as a duty but as a privilege, and holiness not as restriction but as the pathway to divine intimacy.

You will encounter real stories of glory—testimonies of those who walked into boardrooms and watched chains break, entered hospitals and saw the impossible bow, stood in worship and felt the weight of heaven settle. These are not spiritual celebrities. They are nameless warriors who chose to be faithful when no one was looking. And their lives declare a simple truth: God still rests His glory on those who make room for Him.

You will be equipped to live differently—not just on Sundays, but every day. In your workplace, at your dinner table, on the commute, in your conversations. Manifesting the glory is not about being spooky—it is about being so full of God that everything around you must respond. Darkness cannot remain where glory dwells. Fear cannot thrive where presence abides. This is not hype. It is holy. And it is possible.

God is not hiding. He is searching. The eyes of the Lord roam to and fro across the earth, looking for hearts fully His (2 Chronicles 16:9). He is not looking for perfect vessels. He is looking for surrendered ones. He is not looking for talent. He is looking for trust. If He can find people willing to crucify their pride, cleanse their hands, and purify their motives, He will mark them with glory.

This book is your invitation. Not just to learn, but to become. Not just to read, but to respond. The pages ahead are not steps to success; they are altars of surrender. Lay down what must die, and watch what God raises. Let your life become the tabernacle where heaven meets earth.

This is not a concept—it is a calling. A calling to become what you were always designed to be: a glory carrier. A vessel of weighty presence. A walking encounter. A living witness that God still dwells among men.

Do not read this book to be inspired. Read it to be transformed. Let it provoke the cry in your spirit that says, "Lord, I will not move without Your glory." And as you walk this journey, may the fire of God fall afresh upon your altar. May your life burn bright in the darkness. May you carry Him so deeply that the world cannot ignore the fragrance you leave behind.

This is your moment. Not to be seen, but to shine. Not for applause, but for impact. Not to build a name, but to reveal His. The glory is not for you—it is through you. And the world is waiting to behold it.

Chapter 1: The Weight of Glory

There is something unexplainable that happens when the glory of God enters a room. It is not hype or emotion. It is not theatrics or noise. It is the kind of presence that silences conversations, buckles knees, and fills the air with holy fear. You can feel it in your bones. You can hear it in your spirit. It is as if heaven leans close and the natural gives way to the supernatural. The room does not just shift—it is saturated. And yet, this glory is not confined to revival tents or upper room gatherings. It is meant to walk with you. It is meant to rest upon you. It is meant to be carried into hospitals, classrooms, buses, and board meetings. But before it can be carried, it must be understood.

The Hebrew word for glory is *kabod*, which means "weight" or "heaviness." It is not a metaphorical weight; it is a spiritual reality. The glory of God is not an accessory to His presence—it is the full expression of His character, His authority, His holiness, and His majesty. When the glory comes, everything not rooted in Him begins to tremble. When Isaiah saw the glory, he cried out, "Woe is me! I am undone!" (Isaiah 6:5). This is the kind of glory that does not flatter—it exposes. It does not entertain—it transforms.

When Moses descended from Mount Sinai after forty days in God's presence, his face shone so brightly that the people were afraid to come near him (Exodus 34:29–30). He did not ask for it. He did not earn it. He simply absorbed what he beheld. The weight of God's glory had left a mark on his countenance. This is what happens when humans encounter the divine. They cannot leave unchanged. The glory always leaves evidence.

David understood the power and weight of glory as well. When he tried to transport the Ark of the Covenant on a cart, it led to tragedy. Uzzah reached out to steady the Ark and fell dead (2 Samuel 6:6–7). Why? Because the presence of God was never meant to be carried by human invention—it was meant to rest on sanctified shoulders. David later realized that the Ark must be carried on the shoulders of consecrated priests, not on a cart of convenience. The glory demands order. It does not rest casually; it rests carefully.

There is a reason the early church carried such power. They were not chasing crowds or platforms. They were hosting glory. Peter's shadow healed the sick—not because of a technique, but because he walked so closely with God that his nearness caused the spiritual atmosphere to bend. It was not Peter who was great. It was the glory he carried that made everything submit. The presence that overshadowed Mary and caused the Word to become flesh is the same glory that now lives inside every Spirit-filled believer. The question is not whether we have access to glory. The question is whether we have made room for it.

Glory is not light. It is weight. It does not float. It presses. It presses on your thoughts, your will, your pride, your flesh. It demands surrender, not speed. In a world obsessed with momentum, glory asks you to pause. It asks you to kneel. It asks you to decrease so that Christ may increase. It interrupts schedules and wrecks agendas. It does not fit in neatly—it takes over. This is why it is rare. Because many want the benefits of glory without bearing the burden of consecration. But God does not give His glory cheaply. He entrusts it to those who tremble at His Word, who honor His presence, and who have been crushed until only Christ remains.

In 1906, a small mission on Azusa Street became the epicenter of a global revival. Eyewitnesses described the glory of God as a physical cloud that filled the room. Children would play in it. The sick would be healed under it. And people would fall on their faces, not out of emotional frenzy, but because they sensed the weight of holiness pressing in. One visitor reported that even before stepping through the doors, the atmosphere gripped his soul. He said, "It felt like stepping into another world." That is what happens when glory dwells among people—it creates holy ground in the most unlikely places.

And yet, even the Azusa revival faded. Not because God's glory diminished, but because people lost the awe. They became familiar with what should have made them tremble. They stopped stewarding the weight and began to merchandise the wonder. This is the danger of glory without fear—when we touch holy things with unholy hands, the result is not power, but judgment. Ananias and Sapphira learned this in Acts 5. In the glory, even lies are lethal. There was no space for casual deception in a place so filled with

God. The same Spirit that heals is the Spirit that exposes. The same presence that brings joy brings justice.

The weight of glory is not just for gatherings. It is for living. It should be seen in how we forgive, how we parent, how we speak, how we give, and how we carry ourselves when no one is watching. Glory is not goosebumps—it is governance. It is when God's rule overtakes our rebellion. It is when His thoughts become our thoughts, and His will becomes our default. It is when we become so aware of His nearness that sin becomes unthinkable, not because of fear, but because of love.

But glory is not instantaneous. It is cultivated. It is invited through honor and retained through obedience. Many pray, "Lord, show me Your glory," but they forget that God showed Moses His glory only after Moses was willing to be hidden in the cleft of a rock. Glory comes to those who are willing to be hidden. It does not rest on performers—it rests on worshippers. It does not fall on the loudest—it falls on the purest. And when it comes, it stays only where it is valued.

History records that Smith Wigglesworth once entered a train compartment and sat quietly. Without preaching a sermon, without saying a word, a man across the cabin began to weep and cry out, "You convict me of sin!" What was it? Not charisma. Not conversation. It was glory. It was the weight of heaven resting on a surrendered man. That same glory is available today. It is not reserved for preachers. It is not limited to conferences. It longs to dwell in living rooms, coffee shops, and sidewalks. But it will only rest where it is welcomed.

Carrying glory requires internal transformation. It requires humility, hunger, and holiness. It requires that we stop measuring ourselves by worldly metrics and start seeking heaven's approval. It is not about visibility—it is about availability. God is not looking for talent. He is looking for temples. He is looking for hearts that are clean, hands that are open, and spirits that are undivided. When He finds them, He fills them. And when He fills them, the world begins to see a glimpse of heaven on earth.

The glory of God is the answer to every crisis. It is the solution for every broken system. It is the healing balm for every wounded soul. But it will not come through clever ideas or strategic plans. It will come through laid-down lives. Through those who are willing to be misunderstood, overlooked, and even rejected, if it means being carriers of God. Because once you have tasted the glory, nothing else satisfies. No stage, no applause, no success, no title. Only Him.

This chapter is not an invitation to study glory. It is a call to seek it. To cry out like Moses did—not for a blessing, but for the very face of God. To be ruined for the ordinary. To be ruined for anything less than the tangible presence of the King of Glory. Because when He comes, everything changes. And when you carry Him, everything around you must adjust to His presence.

The weight of glory is not burdensome—it is beautiful. It is not oppressive—it is freeing. It does not push you down—it lifts you up. It does not diminish your identity—it reveals your purpose. You were not created to live lightly. You were made to carry something eternal, something holy, something that makes darkness flee and dead things come alive.

You were made to carry glory.

Chapter 2: Christ in You, the Hope of Glory

The most stunning mystery ever revealed to humanity was not hidden in a mountain or sealed in a scroll. It was concealed in a Person. When the Apostle Paul wrote to the Colossians, he did not merely offer encouragement; he delivered a revelation so profound that it shook the foundations of religion and redefined what it means to be human. "To them God chose to make known how great among the Gentiles are the riches of the glory of this mystery," he wrote, "which is Christ in you, the hope of glory" (Colossians 1:27). Those words were not poetic sentiment. They were explosive truth. The glory mankind had lost in Eden was not just restored—it was placed within.

This revelation stands at the heart of the gospel. The incarnation did not end with Jesus walking the streets of Galilee. The glory that once hovered over the Ark, that made mountains tremble, that caused prophets to fall face down, now lives inside every believer. This is not theological theory. It is divine reality. When Christ ascended, He did not leave us empty. He sent the Spirit to indwell, empower, and transform. The glory is not something to chase—it is Someone who resides within.

To understand the magnitude of this truth, one must consider what was required to make it possible. The veil that once separated man from God was torn—not from bottom to top, but from top to bottom (Matthew 27:51). Heaven made the first move. The separation was not bridged by human effort but by divine sacrifice. The blood of Christ did not merely cover sin; it cleansed the vessel, making it fit for divine habitation. This is why the glory could now enter where it had never entered before—not into a temple built with hands, but into human hearts washed by mercy.

When Stephen, the first martyr, stood before his accusers, the Scripture says his face looked like the face of an angel (Acts 6:15). He was not glowing from fear or defiance. He was radiant because of who lived within him. As stones were hurled at his body, he saw the heavens open and the Son of Man standing at the right hand of God. That kind of clarity in the midst of cruelty does not come from willpower. It comes from glory. Christ in him was not a doctrine—it was his source of life, hope, and courage.

Carrying Christ within does not mean life will be easy. It means life will be anchored. When Paul and Silas were beaten and chained in prison, they did not weep—they worshipped. Not because they enjoyed suffering, but because they were possessed by a greater presence. The glory within them was not silenced by chains. It erupted in praise. And the earth responded. The prison shook. Doors opened. Captives were set free. This is what happens when Christ is not just acknowledged but enthroned within. Circumstances may confine the body, but they cannot imprison the glory.

The hope of glory is not wishful thinking. It is the confident expectation of a life infused with divine power, truth, and presence. It is the assurance that we are never alone, never abandoned, never without access to heaven's resources. Hope is not a passive posture. It is a bold stance. It declares that no matter what surrounds us, something greater resides in us. The world sees crisis. We see opportunity. The world feels fear. We manifest peace. The world expects breakdown. We carry breakthrough. Not because of who we are—but because of who He is in us.

But this glory is not automatic. While the indwelling Christ is a gift, the manifestation of His glory depends on yieldedness. Many have Christ within but live as if He is absent. They silence His voice, ignore His prompting, and resist His leading. Glory is not dormant—it is often suppressed by disobedience, pride, and compromise. The same Paul who declared the mystery also prayed that Christ would dwell in our hearts "through faith" (Ephesians 3:17). Not visit. Dwell. Not be mentioned. Be magnified. Christ will not share space with idols. His presence demands priority.

The early church did not spread because of strategy. It spread because of presence. Fishermen became reformers. Tax collectors became evangelists. Former prostitutes became preachers. Not through self-improvement, but through divine indwelling. They did not merely believe in Jesus—they carried Him. Every city they entered felt the impact. Demons cried out. Religious systems were disrupted. Entire households were saved. They did not bring a message alone—they brought a person. And that person was the glory of God in human form.

There was a woman in the city of Philippi—a seller of purple—whose heart the Lord opened through the message of Paul. Her conversion led to the formation of the first church in Europe. But behind the words Paul spoke was the weight of who was speaking through him. This is the distinction between persuasive speech and piercing truth. When Christ speaks through a yielded vessel, hearts open. Chains fall. Resistance melts. This is not talent. This is glory.

Yet, many today live beneath this reality. They strive for relevance but lack reverence. They chase affirmation but avoid transformation. They want visibility but neglect intimacy. And so the glory within remains hidden—like treasure buried in a field. But it was never meant to be buried. It was meant to be revealed. Jesus declared, "Let your light shine before others" (Matthew 5:16). He was not calling us to manufacture light. He was calling us to release what has already been deposited. The Spirit within us is not quiet—He is waiting. Waiting for surrendered hearts that say, "Not my will, but Yours be done."

The Samaritan woman at the well encountered more than a man—she encountered the glory of God in flesh. Her shame could not hide it. Her past could not resist it. Her theology could not contain it. And when she drank of that living water, she became a witness, a vessel, a voice. The same woman who once avoided crowds became a herald of truth. Glory transformed her. Not from the outside in—but from the inside out.

This is the power of Christ in you. It is not a feeling. It is not a phase. It is a Person whose presence changes everything. He will not merely comfort—He will confront. He will not simply visit—He will take over. He will turn complacency into conviction, routine into revelation, and weakness into worship. His glory is not seasonal. It is eternal. And when it is given room, it will not just touch you—it will transform those around you.

There are men and women even now in quiet places around the world who carry this glory without fame or recognition. They do not seek platforms. They seek purity. They do not boast in gifts. They bear fruit. Their names may never be known to the world, but their lives shake the heavens. Why? Because Christ in them is not a doctrine—it is a dwelling. They live in Him, and He lives in them. And the result is unmistakable: they shine.

The world does not need more personalities. It needs more presence. It needs believers who have ceased performing and started carrying. It needs those who have allowed Christ to be formed in them—not just believed, but obeyed; not just worshipped, but followed. It needs people whose lives are not defined by their struggles, but by their surrender. This is the distinguishing mark of a glory carrier. Not perfection, but possession.

You may feel weak. You may feel unqualified. But the glory is not about you. It is about who lives in you. Gideon felt unworthy. Jeremiah felt too young. Moses felt inadequate. But none of their insecurities outweighed the power of divine indwelling. God does not choose based on pedigree. He chooses based on posture. A surrendered heart is His favorite resting place.

There is a reason Paul called it a mystery. Because it makes no sense in the natural. That the God of creation would choose to dwell in jars of clay. That eternity would inhabit mortality. That the Almighty would live in the weak. But this is the wonder of grace. This is the miracle of the gospel. That the very glory that once hovered over the mercy seat now lives in hearts made new. Not because we deserved it, but because mercy made room.

You do not need to ascend a mountain to meet with God. You need only to acknowledge who lives inside of you. You are not waiting for glory—you are hosting it. You are not chasing presence—you are carrying it. And when you live with that awareness, everything changes. Temptation loses its appeal. Fear loses its grip. Life gains eternal weight.

Let this truth settle deep within: Christ in you is the hope of glory. Not a theory. Not a symbol. A Person. A King. A Savior. A fire that cannot be quenched. He is not far. He is near. He is not dormant. He is alive. And He is waiting for vessels who will believe, yield, and walk as if heaven lives within them.

Let the mystery become your reality.

Chapter 3: The Glory Carriers of Scripture

Throughout the pages of Scripture, certain men and women emerge not merely as historical figures, but as divine conduits—individuals upon whom the presence of God rested with unmistakable weight. These were not perfect people. They were not always eloquent or qualified. But they shared one trait that marked their lives and altered history: they carried the glory. And they did not carry it for applause or admiration. They bore it for purpose. They became evidence that God was not distant, but near—actively working through yielded vessels to accomplish His will on earth.

When Abraham left Ur, he was not given a detailed itinerary—only a promise. Yet he obeyed, and as he walked, altars rose. Wherever he pitched his tent, he built places for worship. Glory rested on the one who obeyed without full understanding. Abraham's journey was not just geographic— it was generational. He carried more than faith; he carried a covenant. And from his obedience, nations were born, blessings flowed, and heaven's intention unfolded on earth.

Moses encountered the glory in a burning bush, but that was not the end—it was the beginning. What set him apart was not the miracle he saw but the posture he took. He turned aside. He paid attention. He removed his sandals and listened. In a world addicted to speed, Moses slowed down—

and glory met him there. Later, on Mount Sinai, he would ascend into fire and return with a face so radiant that it had to be veiled. Moses did not just talk to God. He carried God's voice, God's law, and God's glory into the midst of a rebellious people. And even after miracles, he still cried, "Show me Your glory" (Exodus 33:18). He was not content with manifestations. He longed for the face.

Joshua carried the glory not through charisma but through consistency. He lingered in the tent of meeting even after Moses departed. He did not seek promotion—he sought presence. And when it was time to lead, he did not rely on strategy alone. He led priests to carry the Ark into a flooded river, and the waters parted. The same presence that marked Moses now moved with Joshua—not because of a mantle, but because of his posture.

The prophets understood the cost of carrying glory. Elijah did not merely call down fire; he lived in separation. He confronted kings, endured famine, and hid in caves. The weight of glory often meant the absence of applause. Yet when he prayed, fire fell, and the hearts of a nation turned back to God. He did not manipulate atmospheres—he hosted one. Elisha, his successor, asked for a double portion of his spirit, and it was given—not because he was bold, but because he followed to the end. From plowing fields to parting rivers, he walked under an open heaven because he refused to let go of what he knew was worth the cost.

David's life offers a portrait of glory wrapped in humanity. He was not the tallest or most likely, yet he was chosen. Not because of his appearance, but because of his heart. The glory rested on a shepherd boy who wrote psalms in fields and trusted God in caves. When the Ark of the Covenant returned to Jerusalem, David danced with abandon. He did not care about dignity—he cared about presence. His worship was not a performance; it was a response to glory. Though he stumbled, he never stopped seeking. Though he sinned, he never stopped repenting. This is the paradox of glory carriers: they are flawed, but they are desperate.

Isaiah saw the Lord high and lifted up, and the train of His robe filled the temple. The foundations shook. The thresholds trembled. And Isaiah cried out, "Woe is me, for I am undone!" (Isaiah 6:5). Glory will always undress pride. It reveals what masks cannot hide. Yet it also commissions. After the coal touched his lips, Isaiah was sent. Glory does not just cleanse—it compels. It makes cowards into messengers. It makes orphans into ambassadors.

Ezekiel's visions were otherworldly. Wheels within wheels, creatures full of eyes, rivers flowing from the temple. He was not writing fantasy—he was describing glory. The glory of God filled the temple with a brilliance and weight that words could scarcely contain. But later, he saw the glory depart. This is perhaps the most sobering truth: glory can leave. When idolatry enters and reverence is lost, the cloud lifts. What once was sacred becomes routine. What once made people tremble now becomes merchandise. But Ezekiel also prophesied its return. The glory of the Lord will once again fill His house—not made with hands, but hearts made holy.

In the New Testament, everything changes—but the glory intensifies. The Word becomes flesh and dwells among us. And we beheld His glory—glory as of the only Son from the Father, full of grace and truth (John 1:14). Jesus was not merely anointed—He was glory incarnate. When He touched the leper, purity flowed in reverse. When He walked into villages, demons shrieked. When He spoke, the winds obeyed. But what set Him apart was not just power—it was surrender. He carried glory because He walked in perfect alignment with the Father. "I do nothing on My own," He said (John 5:19). Glory followed submission.

At the Mount of Transfiguration, the veil lifted. His face shone like the sun, and His clothes became white as light. Peter, James, and John saw the divine nature break through the human frame. And they wanted to build tents—to remain. But Jesus led them back down. Because glory is not for seclusion—it is for transformation. The mountain prepares you for the mission. And Jesus' mission was not just to display glory but to deposit it. Through His death and resurrection, He would make a way for that same glory to rest upon those who believed.

The early church was born not with programs, but with power. In the upper room, a sound like a mighty rushing wind filled the place. Tongues of fire appeared. And they were all filled with the Holy Spirit. What had once rested upon the tabernacle now rested on people. The glory had found a new dwelling—men and women who would carry it into the streets. Peter stood and preached, and three thousand were cut to the heart. Not because of eloquence, but because of glory.

Stephen, full of grace and power, performed wonders among the people. When falsely accused, he did not defend himself. He saw the heavens opened. And even as stones flew, his face radiated. Glory does not always preserve life—but it always magnifies Christ. Paul, once a persecutor, encountered the risen Jesus on the road to Damascus. The light was so bright it blinded him. And from that moment, he carried a weight that no prison could confine. Shipwrecks, beatings, rejections—none of it stopped the advance of glory. Because glory is not limited by surroundings. It thrives in surrender.

Even women like Mary, the mother of Jesus, bore glory in ways the world could not see. She carried the Messiah in her womb, not by effort, but by yielding. "Let it be to me according to your word," she said (Luke 1:38). That is the heart of every glory carrier: surrender before strategy. When she visited Elizabeth, the child in her cousin's womb leapt. Glory always causes a reaction. It cannot be hidden. It cannot be silenced. It causes what is dormant to move. Even in wombs.

There were no microphones in the upper room. No platforms. No spotlights. But there was glory. And that glory turned cowards into bold witnesses, skeptics into saints, and enemies into evangelists. It has not faded. It has not weakened. The same glory that split the sea, filled the temple, overshadowed the virgin, and fell at Pentecost is still moving today. But it looks for carriers. Not containers. Containers store. Carriers release.

The glory of God is not nostalgic. It is not a relic of the past. It is the present expression of an eternal King, looking for bodies to dwell in, mouths to speak through, and hands to work with. You were not born in this generation by accident. You are not reading these words by coincidence. Just as God called Moses, Elijah, Mary, and Paul—He is calling you. Not to repeat their stories, but to live your own. To walk so closely with Him that when you enter a room, heaven walks in too.

The glory did not depart with the apostles. It was never meant to fade. It was meant to spread. From Jerusalem to the ends of the earth. From pulpits to coffee shops. From sanctuaries to schools. But it will only rest where it is honored. Only on those who carry the posture of ancient carriers: humility, hunger, and holiness. It is not complicated. But it is costly.

There is no shortage of talent in the church today. No shortage of programs, content, or innovation. But what the world waits for is what it has always waited for: the glory. The manifest presence of God flowing through surrendered lives. The kind that makes kings bow and sinners repent. The kind that lifts the broken and silences the proud. The kind that does not just visit—but dwells.

The glory is calling. And history is watching. Will you carry it?

Chapter 4: Created for Glory

Before the first star was set in motion or a single mountain rose from the deep, glory existed. Not as an idea, but as the eternal atmosphere surrounding God Himself. Glory was not made. Glory is. It is the uncontainable expression of His nature—the splendor of His holiness, the brilliance of His power, the weight of His being. When God chose to create mankind, He was not looking for entertainment. He was not lonely. He was revealing Himself. He was crafting a creature that would carry His image and reflect His glory.

The origin of humanity is not found in the dust alone but in the breath that entered it. "Then the Lord God formed the man of dust from the ground and breathed into his nostrils the breath of life" (Genesis 2:7). The breath was not air. It was life. Spirit. Glory. God did not merely make man to exist—He made man to represent. In a world freshly formed, filled with color, sound, and beauty, the crowning act of creation was not a galaxy. It was a man. A man made to walk with God, talk with God, rule under God, and reveal God.

When God said, "Let us make man in our image, after our likeness" (Genesis 1:26), He was not speaking casually. He was issuing a decree. That man and woman would be His representatives on earth—governing with delegated authority, stewarding creation, and walking in fellowship with their Creator. This image was not physical. It was spiritual. It was the glory of God etched into human existence. The psalmist would later marvel, "What is man that you are mindful of him?... You have crowned him with glory and honor" (Psalm 8:4–5).

Adam and Eve were not created to survive. They were designed to reflect. Every action they took, every word they spoke, every step they walked was meant to radiate the nature of the One who made them. There was no division between the sacred and the secular. All of life was sacred because all of life was lived in the presence of glory. Work was worship. Walking was communion. Naming animals was prophetic stewardship. They were not laboring for identity—they were living from glory.

But something happened. Not because of an external assault, but because of an internal decision. They listened to a lie that questioned God's goodness and distorted His word. The serpent offered what they already possessed—godlikeness. But instead of receiving through relationship, they attempted to take through rebellion. And in that moment, the glory lifted. The covering vanished. And for the first time, shame entered. Not because they were naked, but because they had been stripped of what clothed them from the beginning—God's presence.

Sin did not simply make man bad. It made him barren. Empty of glory. Hollow in purpose. Separated from the source of life. The fall was not just a moral failure. It was a glory loss. Romans 3:23 echoes this eternal consequence: "For all have sinned and fall short of the glory of God." The tragedy is not just in sinning. It is in falling short of the glory we were made for. Glory is not an accessory to life—it is the essence of it. When it departs, chaos enters. Identity fractures. Creation groans. And mankind forgets who he is.

But God never abandoned His purpose. His image would not be erased. His glory would not remain distant. From the very beginning, He clothed the guilty with animal skins—foreshadowing a covering that would one day restore what was lost. He called Abraham from a pagan land, not to build a nation only, but to bless all nations. He delivered Israel from Egypt, not just for freedom's sake, but so His glory could dwell among them again. The tabernacle, the ark, the sacrifices—all were signposts pointing to something greater. God was not content to be above. He longed to be among.

The prophets saw glimpses. Isaiah saw His train filling the temple. Ezekiel saw a throne with fire and wheels and radiance. But they also saw the people turning away, choosing idols over intimacy. They wept as the glory departed, not because of what was taken, but because of what was forfeited. Yet through tears, a promise emerged. That one day, the glory would return—not in a cloud, but in a person.

And then He came.

Not in splendor, but in swaddling cloths. Not in thunder, but in the cry of a newborn. John writes, "The Word became flesh and dwelt among us, and we have seen His glory" (John 1:14). The glory returned, not to the temple, but to humanity. In Jesus, the original design was restored. He walked as Adam never could—sinless, surrendered, saturated with the Spirit. He did not just show us how to live—He showed us who we were meant to be.

Jesus carried glory not just in miracles, but in moments. When He touched the outcast, glory healed. When He wept over Lazarus, glory wept. When He washed feet, glory stooped low. And when He hung on the cross, the world saw something it had never seen before—glory wrapped in suffering. For in that moment, He bore our sin, our shame, our fallenness—and made a way for glory to return to its rightful place.

The resurrection was not the end—it was the beginning of a new creation. Jesus, the firstborn among many, rose not just to conquer death, but to reestablish man as a carrier of glory. And fifty days later, in an upper room, the promise exploded. Fire rested on heads. Languages broke out. Fear fled. And the Spirit came. Not to visit, but to dwell. Not to hover, but to inhabit.

We were created for glory. Redeemed for glory. Filled with glory. This is not a poetic idea. It is a divine reality. Every believer who receives Christ receives not just salvation, but restoration. The image begins to reform. The likeness is reignited. We begin to be transformed "from one degree of glory to another" (2 Corinthians 3:18). This is not self-help. This is Spirit transformation. The same power that raised Jesus now lives in those who believe.

But glory is not passive. It demands participation. We must walk by the Spirit. We must crucify the flesh. We must renew the mind. Because the more room we give Him, the more His nature is seen in us. Not perfection, but progression. Not pretending, but becoming. Every act of obedience reveals glory. Every moment of worship reflects it. Every decision to forgive, to love, to serve, to yield—these are not small things. They are reflections of divine design.

There is a lie that says only some people are called. That only ministers, prophets, or missionaries carry the glory. But the truth is this: if Christ dwells in you, so does His glory. Whether you are raising children, building houses, writing books, teaching students, or driving buses—glory goes with you. The Spirit does not divide life into spiritual and secular. All of it is His. All of it can reveal Him.

Creation is still groaning. Still waiting. Not for better ideas or louder arguments. But for the sons and daughters of God to be revealed (Romans 8:19). Not just as churchgoers, but as glory bearers. As those who walk into broken places and bring healing. Who enter dark rooms and bring light. Who face impossible odds and do not flinch—because they know who lives in them.

You were not made to mimic the world. You were made to reflect the King. The glory you carry is not ornamental—it is essential. It is the evidence of His indwelling. The world does not need imitation. It needs incarnation. It needs people who have been with God and walk in His ways. Who do not need a stage to shine, but carry presence wherever they go.

There is a dignity in your design. You are not random. You are not accidental. You are not a problem to be fixed—you are a vessel to be filled. Your hands were meant to heal. Your words were meant to create. Your life was meant to reveal. Glory is not something you earn. It is something you yield to. And the more you yield, the more you reflect the One who made you.

This is your calling. Not just to go to heaven, but to bring heaven wherever you go. Not just to avoid sin, but to radiate holiness. Not just to believe in God, but to become like Him. You are being transformed into His image. Not just morally. Glory does not make you religious. It makes you radiant.

The journey is not always easy. There are days when you will feel anything but glorious. But feelings do not determine truth. The Spirit within you does not fluctuate with your emotions. He remains. He strengthens. He transforms. And He will finish what He began. Because He is faithful, and He is forming Christ in you.

Lift your eyes. Remember who you are. You were not made for bondage. You were not made for shame. You were not made to blend in. You were created for glory.

Live like it.

Chapter 5: Glory Lost, Glory Restored

The ache of humanity is not primarily rooted in lack of provision, comfort, or opportunity. It is rooted in the memory of what was lost. Deep within every soul is the residue of Eden—a faint, persistent longing for the intimacy, purpose, and glory that once defined life before the fall. We were not created to live disconnected from our source. But sin fractured the connection. And when the connection broke, the glory left. Not because God rejected man, but because man rejected God.

In the beginning, there was no divide. Adam and Eve did not have to seek the presence of God—it was their natural environment. His voice was not foreign; it was familiar. There was no shame in His gaze, no fear in His footsteps. The glory was not a distant force. It was their atmosphere. It clothed them. It filled them. It defined them. There was no need for titles or roles. They were known, and they knew. That is what glory does. It restores identity. It reveals design. It anchors worth.

But temptation entered not through violence, but through suggestion. The serpent did not attack with force; he planted a question. "Did God actually say…?" (Genesis 3:1). It was subtle, strategic, and aimed not just at God's command but at His character. Doubt was the doorway. Pride was the motive. Disobedience was the act. And the consequence was catastrophic. When Adam and Eve reached for what was forbidden, they did not become like God—they became alienated from Him. And the first thing they noticed was not their sin. It was their nakedness.

Shame is always the first sign of lost glory. It rushes in when presence departs. It whispers lies about worth. It drives us to cover what was never meant to be hidden. And it causes us to run from the very voice that once gave us life. Adam and Eve hid among the trees, as if foliage could shield them from omniscience. The tragedy was not that they sinned. It was that they no longer trusted the One who could restore them. That is the power of shame. It not only exposes—it isolates.

God's response, however, was not wrathful abandonment. He came looking. "Where are you?" He asked—not because He lacked information, but because He desired restoration. He already knew. But He wanted them to know He had not withdrawn His pursuit. This is the mercy of God. He steps into the aftermath, not to destroy, but to redeem. He covers their shame with garments made from sacrifice—a foreshadowing of the Lamb who would one day take away the sin of the world.

The narrative of Scripture from that moment forward is the story of glory in pursuit of restoration. From the blood-stained doorposts in Egypt to the cloud by day and the fire by night, God kept drawing near. The Ark of the Covenant, though housed in tents and temples, was never about furniture—it was about fellowship. The sacrifices, the feasts, the priesthood—all were temporary scaffolds meant to point to a greater plan. They could manage sin, but they could not remove it. They could display glory, but they could not restore it.

One of the most haunting moments in the Old Testament is found in Ezekiel's vision. The prophet watches as the glory of the Lord departs from the temple (Ezekiel 10). It hovers. It hesitates. And then it lifts. Slowly. Tragically. It is a picture of what happens when God's presence is taken for granted, when idolatry fills the inner courts, and when routine replaces reverence. The people still had the temple, the rituals, the form—but the weight was gone. And with it, protection, power, and purpose.

Yet even in exile, God did not forget His promise. Through tears and lamentation, He whispered hope. That one day, He would give a new heart, a new spirit. That His glory would return—not to buildings, but to people. Not to systems, but to sons and daughters. This hope was not wishful thinking. It was anchored in covenant. And it pointed forward to a moment that would change everything.

When the angel appeared to the shepherds outside Bethlehem, he did not just bring a message. He brought glory. "And the glory of the Lord shone around them, and they were filled with great fear" (Luke 2:9). The announcement was more than a birth—it was a declaration: glory has returned. Not in a cloud, but in a child. Not above, but among. The Word had become flesh. The invisible had become visible. The glory that once walked with Adam was now swaddled in humanity.

Jesus did not merely restore what was lost—He revealed what was possible. He healed, not just to show compassion, but to reveal what glory does when it touches brokenness. He forgave sins to prove that presence had returned. He walked in authority because He walked in unity with the Father. Every miracle, every teaching, every act of mercy was glory in motion. And when He went to the cross, He did not lose the glory—He offered it.

On the cross, the veil tore. The barrier that symbolized separation was removed. Not just in the temple, but in the spirit. Glory no longer needed a golden box or a high priest's ritual. It had found a new dwelling place—hearts cleansed by blood, filled by Spirit. The resurrection confirmed what the cross accomplished: sin was broken, shame was disarmed, and glory was on the move.

Pentecost was not a new religion being formed. It was Eden being restored. Fire fell, not to consume, but to commission. Languages erupted, not to confuse, but to unify. What was lost in Genesis began to be reclaimed in Acts. Ordinary people became carriers of extraordinary presence. Not because they mastered theology, but because they surrendered completely.

The restoration of glory is not just about spiritual experiences. It is about transformed existence. It means walking through valleys with peace that defies understanding. It means facing temptation with power that overcomes. It means loving enemies, forgiving offenders, and bearing fruit that no storm can uproot. Glory is not a glow—it is a government. When it returns, it rules.

Paul, once a persecutor of the church, understood this restoration intimately. After encountering the risen Christ, he declared, "We have this treasure in jars of clay" (2 Corinthians 4:7). The treasure was not wisdom, gifting, or knowledge. It was glory. The very presence of God living inside broken, imperfect vessels. This is the mystery of the gospel: that fallen humanity can now host eternal divinity. Not because of merit, but because of mercy.

But restoration is not automatic. It must be received. It must be stewarded. It must be guarded. Just as Adam lost the glory through disobedience, believers today can grieve the Spirit through compromise. That is why Scripture warns not to quench the Spirit, not to ignore His voice, not to treat His presence lightly. Restoration is a gift, but intimacy is a choice.

The restored glory comes with responsibility. It compels us to live differently. To speak with truth, to walk in humility, to pursue purity, and to resist conformity. We are no longer products of the fall—we are carriers of the restoration. The old has gone. The new has come. And the world, though it may not understand it, is waiting for it.

This is why Jesus called us the light of the world. Not a light we produce, but a light we reflect. The same glory that once illuminated Moses' face now radiates through every believer who walks in communion with Christ. And this light is not dimmed by opposition. It shines brightest in darkness. It heals, convicts, restores, and draws. It is not loud—but it is unmistakable.

Restoration means the Church is no longer a place we visit. It is who we are. Wherever believers gather in His name, glory dwells. Whether in cathedrals or living rooms, jungles or cities—the presence of God fills yielded hearts. There is no special breed of person that qualifies. Only the humble, the hungry, the surrendered.

The final picture painted in Scripture is not of a distant heaven or a fearful ending. It is of glory fully restored. A new heaven. A new earth. A city with no temple—because the Lord God Almighty and the Lamb are its temple (Revelation 21:22). No need for sun or moon—because the glory of God gives it light. What began in a garden ends in a city. What was lost is fully restored.

But until that day, we live in the now and not yet. We carry the glory in earthen vessels. We fight distractions, wrestle the flesh, and face battles. But we do so from victory, not for it. The veil is torn. The access is granted. The Spirit is given. And the glory is returning—day by day, moment by moment, glory to glory.

Do not live beneath your calling. Do not settle for a form of godliness that lacks power. The glory has been restored. Not just to visit you, but to live in you. You were never meant to carry shame. You were never meant to walk alone. You were made for glory. And that glory has been given back.

Receive it. Guard it. Live it.

Chapter 6: Flesh and Glory Cannot Coexist

There is a reason the glory of God does not rest on every believer the same way. It is not that God plays favorites. It is not because some people are naturally more spiritual. It is because glory has requirements. The presence of God is not something that can be mingled with carnality, selfishness, or pride. Glory demands death to the flesh. Where self reigns, glory withdraws. Where sin is tolerated, presence is grieved. Where the flesh thrives, the Spirit is stifled.

The apostle Paul could not have made it clearer: "Those who are in the flesh cannot please God" (Romans 8:8). He was not speaking only of unbelievers. He was warning the Church that flesh is not just weakness—it is opposition to the Spirit. It resists the things of God. It opposes surrender. It prioritizes comfort, ego, and control. And the glory of God will not rest where it is resisted.

The glory is weighty. It is not decorative—it is transformative. And that transformation begins where the flesh ends. You cannot carry glory while clinging to pride. You cannot walk in presence while protecting your rebellion. You cannot be filled with light while entertaining darkness. Flesh does not just hinder glory—it repels it. This is why, throughout Scripture, every person who was entrusted with the glory first had to undergo a breaking.

Abraham had to leave everything familiar. His homeland. His relatives. His culture. Before he became the father of many nations, he was a man walking in the unknown, guided only by faith. The glory followed obedience, not comfort. Moses spent forty years in the wilderness, stripped of identity, reputation, and ambition, before he could carry the glory of God to Pharaoh's courts. The wilderness did not make him weak—it made him ready. It emptied him of self so that he could be filled with God.

David was anointed king while still smelling like sheep. But the throne did not follow the oil immediately. He was hunted, betrayed, and tested. In caves, not palaces, he learned to crucify the flesh. He learned not to take revenge when opportunity knocked. He learned to worship in obscurity, not just in celebration. And because he refused to let the flesh reign, the glory did.

Jesus Himself, though without sin, fasted for forty days before beginning His ministry. He showed us that the flesh must be subdued even when it is innocent. He denied legitimate hunger to affirm spiritual alignment. And in doing so, He showed the pattern: where the flesh is crucified, the glory flows. The devil offered Him shortcuts—turn stones to bread, jump from the temple, bow for kingdoms. But Jesus responded with the Word, not with impulse. He did not flex power—He submitted to purpose. That is what distinguishes those who carry glory: submission over sensation.

Paul described his own journey with startling transparency. He spoke of a thorn in the flesh—something that kept him dependent, humbled, and grounded. He pleaded with God to remove it. But God responded, "My grace is sufficient for you, for My power is made perfect in weakness" (2 Corinthians 12:9). The glory did not come through Paul's strength. It came through his surrender. And the same is true today.

Flesh is not limited to obvious sins. It can disguise itself in ministry, ambition, and even discipline. It seeks attention. It craves applause. It resists correction. It wants control. And it dies slowly. But if we want to be trusted with glory, we must become enemies of the flesh. We must not pacify it. We must crucify it. Not once, but daily.

Paul wrote, "I die daily" (1 Corinthians 15:31). This was not poetic language. It was the rhythm of his life. Every day, he chose the cross over comfort. Every day, he surrendered his will, his ego, his preferences. And because of that, he carried the glory into cities, prisons, and cultures that had never encountered the living God. He did not need a temple—he was one.

In the tabernacle of Moses, the glory did not rest just anywhere. It fell in the Most Holy Place—behind the veil, on the mercy seat. The outer courts were busy, loud, full of activity. But the glory waited for consecration. The priests had to cleanse themselves, offer sacrifices, and follow divine order. If they bypassed the process, they died. This was not cruelty—it was holiness. The closer one got to the glory, the higher the cost.

Today, many want access to glory without submitting to purification. They want power without prayer. They want anointing without repentance. They want presence without process. But God has not changed. His glory still requires consecration. Not because He is harsh, but because He is holy.

The flesh cannot be managed into submission. It must be crucified. That is why fasting is so essential. It silences the appetites that scream for gratification. It exposes attachments, addictions, and idols. It weakens the outer man so that the inner man can rise. It is not about proving something to God. It is about removing everything that hinders communion with Him.

When believers fast with humility and sincerity, something shifts. The noise of the soul quiets. The Spirit speaks more clearly. The distractions lose their grip. Fasting does not earn glory—it makes room for it. It says, "Lord, I want You more than I want this." It tears down altars to self and builds altars for God.

Prayer does the same. True prayer is not just words—it is surrender. It is not performance—it is presence. It exposes pride, corrects motives, and draws us into alignment. The flesh resists prayer because prayer dethrones the flesh. It forces us to face our need, our brokenness, our emptiness. And in that place, glory comes. Not always with feelings. Not always with fireworks. But with a deep, unshakable awareness that He is here, and He is holy.

Worship is also a weapon against the flesh. Not the kind that entertains or entertains others, but the kind that exalts Him alone. When we worship in spirit and truth, we dethrone ourselves. We lift Him up, not for what He gives, but for who He is. And in that posture, the flesh loses its grip. Pride melts. Self fades. And glory falls.

The Church is full of gifted people who have not yet dealt with the flesh. They speak well, sing well, serve well—but underneath it all, the motives are mixed. The applause is addictive. The influence becomes identity. The platform becomes the goal. And the glory cannot rest on polluted altars. God does not bless what we pretend to surrender. He blesses what we place on the altar, regardless of the cost.

When the glory of God filled Solomon's temple, the priests could not stand to minister (2 Chronicles 5:14). They were overwhelmed. Silenced. Humbled. That is what glory does. It levels pride. It quiets noise. It reminds everyone that this is not about us. This is not our show. This is holy ground. And only the surrendered can stay.

The flesh will always offer alternatives to glory. It will offer entertainment. It will offer control. It will offer success. But none of these can carry the weight of His presence. They may draw crowds, but they do not transform lives. They may stir emotion, but they do not host glory.

This is why revival always begins with repentance. It is not about volume—it is about brokenness. It is not about charisma—it is about contrition. When people weep over sin, turn from compromise, and cry out for holiness, the glory returns. Not because God is reluctant—but because hearts are finally ready.

Every believer has a choice. To feed the flesh or crucify it. To make room for the Spirit or grieve Him. To protect pride or pursue presence. The decision is daily. It is made in private, not on stages. It is forged in prayer, not performance. And it is visible in fruit, not feelings.

God is looking for resting places. Not events, but people. Not noise, but holiness. Not personalities, but purity. He longs to dwell with those who fear Him, love Him, and yield to Him completely. And when He finds such a heart, the glory falls. Not for a moment, but for a lifetime.

Do not be deceived by the illusion of spiritual success. If the flesh is alive, the glory is hindered. If pride reigns, presence departs. If compromise is tolerated, power is diminished. But if the flesh is crucified, the Spirit flows freely. And where the Spirit of the Lord is, there is liberty. There is fire. There is transformation. There is glory.

The cross is not just where Jesus died. It is where the flesh must die daily. It is not a relic—it is a reality. And every time we choose the cross, we make room for the crown. Not a crown of applause, but a crown of glory. A life so surrendered that heaven sees a resting place.

You cannot carry glory and cater to the flesh. One will always silence the other. Choose wisely. Choose surrender. Choose death that leads to life. Because on the other side of crucifixion, there is resurrection. And on the other side of obedience, there is glory.

Chapter 7: The Hidden Power of Fasting

There is a place in the spirit that cannot be accessed through noise, effort, or performance. It cannot be bought, manipulated, or mimicked. It is a sacred place where heaven speaks clearly, power flows freely, and glory rests deeply. But that place is guarded by hunger—not physical, but spiritual. The soul must be emptied before it can be filled. And fasting is the key.

Fasting is one of the most neglected yet powerful disciplines in the believer's life. It is not a diet, a religious badge, or a token of spiritual pride. It is a death sentence to the flesh. It is a declaration of war against complacency, compromise, and distraction. It is the stripping away of lesser appetites to make room for holy obsession. It is the voluntary silencing of the body so that the spirit can speak clearly and listen deeply. And wherever true fasting is embraced, the glory follows.

Jesus did not begin His public ministry with a campaign or a miracle. He began with a fast. Forty days in the wilderness. No crowds. No affirmations. No comforts. Just hunger, testing, and the voice of the Father. It was in that place of deprivation that His identity was tested. "If You are the Son of God..." the tempter whispered (Matthew 4:3). And Jesus answered not with emotion, but with truth. He emerged from the wilderness not weakened, but armed. And from that moment on, demons fled, the sick were healed, and the kingdom advanced. The wilderness fast was not a delay—it was preparation. Fasting forged the vessel for glory.

Fasting has always been a doorway to divine encounter. When Moses ascended Mount Sinai, he did not eat for forty days (Exodus 34:23). He did not fast out of ritual. He fasted because he was consumed by glory. In the presence of God, earthly appetites lose their grip. The soul feasts on what the stomach cannot hold. And when he descended, his face shone. Not because of the fast, but because of the glory that met him in it. The fast had emptied him. God had filled him.

Ezra fasted before leading the people back to Jerusalem, seeking protection and direction from the Lord. Esther called for a national fast before approaching the king to intercede for her people. Daniel fasted for twenty-one days, and the heavens responded with angelic visitation and prophetic clarity. These were not manipulative acts—they were desperate postures. Fasting was never about moving God. It was about moving ourselves into alignment with His purposes.

In each case, the glory of God was revealed after the fast, not before. This is the pattern: consecration precedes manifestation. And fasting is consecration at its most raw. It is the laying down of legitimate needs for a higher necessity. It is saying, "I will not be ruled by my appetite. I will not be led by my cravings. I will be governed by the Spirit."

But fasting does more than create space. It exposes idols. When the body is denied, the heart speaks. Anger rises. Bitterness surfaces. Fear screams. Pride reveals itself. In the silence of fasting, the soul's true condition comes into view. This is why many avoid it. Not because it is physically hard, but because it is spiritually honest. Fasting unmasks. It removes the comfort of distractions and forces the believer to confront what has been hidden behind routine.

And yet, that confrontation is the beginning of healing. When the idols fall, glory fills the room. When the noise fades, the whisper of God becomes thunder. Fasting is not punishment—it is pruning. It does not take life—it gives it. Jesus said, "My food is to do the will of Him who sent Me" (John 4:34). Fasting is a return to that posture. It reorders affections. It purifies motives. It clarifies direction.

There is a mystery in fasting that cannot be taught, only experienced. There are breakthroughs that only come on the other side of empty stomachs and bent knees. Not because God is reluctant, but because the flesh is too loud. In fasting, the believer becomes quiet enough to hear. Still enough to perceive. Weak enough to receive.

Isaiah 58 reveals God's heart about true fasting. The people fasted for appearance, but their hearts were hard. They oppressed workers, quarreled, and pointed fingers. And God rebuked them. "Is not this the fast that I choose," He said, "to loose the bonds of wickedness... to let the oppressed go free?" (Isaiah 58:6). True fasting breaks chains. It softens hearts. It brings justice. It restores relationships. It clothes the naked, feeds the hungry, and shelters the homeless. Fasting that pleases God produces glory that transforms not just the individual, but the environment.

When the Church fasts as it should, glory returns to the streets. Revival history proves this. In the 1949 Hebrides Revival, two elderly women—one blind, the other bent by arthritis—fasted and prayed in their cottage. Their hunger provoked heaven. And the glory of God fell on the island. Bars emptied. Churches filled. The lost wept in fields under conviction before hearing a sermon. There were no celebrities. No promotions. Just fasting, prayer, and glory.

The early church fasted regularly. In Acts 13, they fasted and prayed before sending out Paul and Barnabas. Fasting was not reserved for emergencies—it was embedded in their rhythm. They did not view it as legalism, but as love. It was not burdensome—it was beautiful. Because they knew what many have forgotten: fasting is not a loss of food—it is a gain of focus.

Today, in a world ruled by indulgence and speed, fasting feels foreign. The culture screams, "Feed yourself, satisfy yourself, comfort yourself." But the Spirit whispers, "Deny yourself, follow Me." The flesh resists fasting because it knows fasting leads to glory. The enemy fears a fasting church more than a talented one. Because fasting dismantles pride, shakes systems, and births power.

But fasting must be approached with humility. It is not a means of spiritual superiority. Jesus warned against fasting to be seen. "When you fast," He said, "anoint your head and wash your face" (Matthew 6:17). Fasting is not about attention. It is about affection. It is not a badge—it is a basin.

It lowers us before it lifts us. It cleanses before it commissions.

Even Jesus taught that certain kinds of spiritual resistance can only be broken through prayer and fasting (Mark 9:29). Not because prayer alone is insufficient, but because fasting adds a weight to prayer that pierces darkness more deeply. There are territories, strongholds, and generational curses that crumble only when fasting joins the cry. The devil does not fear religion, but he trembles before consecrated vessels.

Fasting is not just for preachers or prophets. It is for every believer who longs for more. It is for the business owner seeking wisdom. The parent interceding for a wayward child. The student crying out for direction. The congregation hungry for revival. Fasting is not about status. It is about surrender.

Some fast one meal. Others a day. Some abstain from media, distractions, or social activity. The expression may vary, but the heart must be the same: "Lord, I want You more than I want anything else." That cry, when genuine, always draws glory.

Glory comes where hunger lives. Not just hunger for results, but hunger for Him. Fasting makes space for intimacy. It is not just about saying no to food—it is about saying yes to presence. It invites God to fill what food can never satisfy. It trains the spirit to lead and the flesh to follow.

The hidden power of fasting is not in its visibility, but in its fruit. You may not feel different during the fast. But something is happening. Something deep. Hidden. Eternal.

Chains are weakening. Veils are lifting. Foundations are shifting. And when the fast is over, the evidence will be clear—not in weight lost, but in glory gained.

You will hear more clearly. Love more deeply. Obey more quickly. Worship more fully. And you will carry a fragrance that cannot be explained, only discerned. Because fasting births glory. Quietly. Powerfully. Permanently.

This generation does not need more content. It needs more consecration. It needs men and women who will turn down the plate to tune into heaven. Who will give up their craving for comfort to become catalysts of revival. Who will say, "I am not satisfied with crumbs—I want the cloud."

Fasting is the ancient path to modern power. The old key that still opens new doors. It is not outdated. It is not optional. It is the secret that unlocks the glory.

Embrace it. Cherish it. Live it.

Chapter 8: The Glory in Giving

There is a dimension of glory that is only unlocked through giving—not casual charity or transactional generosity, but sacrificial surrender that flows from a heart that reveres the Source of all being. Glory does not dwell in greed. It does not rest within stinginess. The presence of the Divine moves through open hands. The one who gives—not out of surplus, but from a surrendered heart—becomes a vessel that light fills and flows through.

Giving is not just about money; it is about trust. It reveals what we truly believe about the nature of provision—whether abundance comes from ourselves or from something far greater. Glory and giving are eternally connected because both require the same posture: yieldedness. When we give, we do not lose. We align ourselves with a realm where multiplication defies natural laws. In that realm, what leaves your hand does not leave your life—it enters your future and returns in ways only the Divine can orchestrate.

From the beginning, giving was woven into worship. Cain and Abel both brought offerings, but only one was accepted—not for lack of quantity, but because of the heart behind it (Genesis 4:3–5). Abel offered the firstborn of his flock, the best, not leftovers. His gift carried weight, it carried cost, and

God honored it. Cain brought something, but it lacked reverence. There was no glory on it, and so no favor.

The first act of extravagant giving recorded in Scripture came not from a wealthy patriarch, but from a man of promise— Abraham. When called to offer Isaac, Abraham was not merely being tested as a father—he was being tested in trust. Isaac was miracle and future wrapped in flesh. Yet Abraham rose early, prepared the wood, climbed the mountain, laid his son on the altar, lifted the knife, and surrendered his most precious possession. Just before the sacrifice, heaven intervened. A ram appeared. The altar was completed. The glory of obedience echoed through generations. That mountain was forever named "The Lord Will Provide."

Glory rests on altars—not physical ones, but internal ones. No literal sacrifice is demanded, but God does ask for our hearts—our trust—our treasures. Jesus said, "Where your treasure is, there your heart will be also" (Matthew 6:21). He wasn't speaking solely to the wealthy; He was unfolding a principle: giving exposes allegiance. It reveals what we worship, what we prioritize, and where we place our confidence in supply. When we give from a place of trust, glory is released.

Paul described believers in Macedonia who, though scraping by, gave from their own need, joyfully and beyond means (2 Corinthians 8:2–3). Their generosity stemmed from honest, surrendered hearts—not prosperity. And because they gave freely, Paul declared, "God is able to make all grace abound to you… so that you will always have everything you need and may abound in every good work" (2 Corinthians 9:8–11). Their giving became a conduit for glory—not the amount given, but the heart behind it.

Consider George Müller, who cared for orphans without ever fundraising. He prayed, trusted, and lived day to day. In one miraculous moment, the home's mortgage was covered and the food delivered at the precise hour. Not coincidence—but glory following trust.

Jesus watched a widow in the temple drop two small coins—her entire livelihood—and said, "She has put in more than all those who gave out of abundance" (Mark 12:43–44). What mattered wasn't the amount but the cost, the faith, the worship.

When the early church sold everything and pooled resources, "awe came upon every soul, and many wonders and signs were done through the apostles" (Acts 2:43–45). Their giving cleared space in hearts and homes. They didn't pay for miracles; they prepared altars—and glory came.

This kind of giving confronts mammon. Money itself isn't evil, but the love of it is the root of all evils (1 Timothy 6:10). That love often hides, even behind spiritual activity. Generosity confronts that love—it declares, "My Source is not money, but the unseen Giver." Generosity trains the soul to trust, opening vistas of provision, presence, wisdom, power—and, yes, glory.

Giving is an act of worship that demonstrates trust (2 Corinthians 9:7). Jesus said, "Give, and it will be given to you... For with the measure you use, it will be measured back to you" (Luke 6:38). Give mercy and you will receive mercy; give time and it finds its way back; give yourself to sacred purpose and presence will overflow. That is the exchange of the kingdom.

True glory in giving isn't reserved for the privileged. I've encountered hidden heroes—a woman in Uganda who gives half her meager income; a Brazilian couple living on small pensions yet sowing generously into youth ministry; underground believers in Iran pooling resources for sacred texts. These are vessels of glory: not in reputation or abundance, but in surrendered hearts.

If we long to carry divine glory, we must give—not reluctantly, sparingly, or for appearance, but cheerfully, freely, joyfully—expecting God's supernatural work through it. We cannot seek more of the Divine while clinging to what we've been asked to release. Whatever is surrendered is filled with glory. Whatever is held back becomes a weight that blocks it. Glory and greed cannot coexist—one must go.

The call is simple: release. Give with intention, purity, and expectancy—not fixated on return, but on what will flow. Open your hands, and watch as heaven touches your life. Glory will appear—not just above you, but through you.

Because where your treasure is, your heart will be—and when your heart aligns with yours, glory comes to rest.

Chapter 9: Praying Until Something Shifts

Prayer is not a ritual. It is not a polite activity for the religious. It is not a quiet background noise in the life of the believer. Prayer is power. It is divine partnership. It is the meeting place where heaven touches earth and the will of God is invited into the affairs of men. It is the language of dependence, the posture of authority, and the birthing place of glory. But prayer that moves glory is not casual. It is not occasional. It is persistent, tenacious, and unrelenting. It prays until something shifts.

There is a kind of prayer that stirs the atmosphere, silences hell, and draws heaven close. It is not motivated by desperation alone, but by revelation—revelation of God's character, His promises, and His readiness to respond. This kind of prayer does not end when the answer is delayed. It presses deeper. It grows louder. It refuses to be denied. It is the prayer of Jacob at Jabbok, wrestling through the night, saying, "I will not let You go unless You bless me" (Genesis 32:26). And heaven did not rebuke him. Heaven renamed him.

When Hannah cried out for a son in the temple, she was not reciting words. She was groaning from the depths of a soul that knew God could change her story. Eli misunderstood her at first, assuming she was drunk. That is the mark of true intercession—those bound to the flesh will not understand it.

But God heard. And Samuel was born—not just an answer to prayer, but a prophet who would anoint kings. Hannah's persistence produced more than relief—it released glory.

Jesus told the parable of a persistent widow who kept returning to an unjust judge (Luke 18:1–8). She pleaded for justice, and though the judge cared nothing for righteousness, he eventually granted her request because of her persistence. And Jesus said, "Will not God give justice to His elect, who cry to Him day and night?" That parable was not about nagging God—it was about trusting His nature enough to keep coming. Real prayer does not quit. It believes that something shifts every time we speak His name.

The early church understood this. After Peter was thrown into prison, "earnest prayer for him was made to God by the church" (Acts 12:5). They did not gather to complain or speculate—they prayed. Not just for comfort, but for release. And heaven responded. An angel entered the prison, chains fell off, doors opened, and Peter walked out untouched. The intercession of the church moved the hand of God. Not in theory. In reality.

This kind of prayer is not reserved for apostles or prophets. It belongs to the ordinary believer who dares to believe that God still moves when His people pray. James, the half-brother of Jesus, wrote with piercing clarity, "The prayer of a righteous person has great power as it is working" (James 5:16). Not had power. Has power. Present, active, potent. And he pointed to Elijah—a man with a nature like ours—who prayed, and the heavens shut. Then he prayed again, and the heavens opened. The climate obeyed the voice of one man who dared to pray until something shifted.

Glory does not rest where prayer is absent. It cannot. Prayer prepares the ground. It sanctifies the atmosphere. It tills the heart. When Jesus cleansed the temple, He declared, "My house shall be called a house of prayer" (Matthew 21:13). Not a house of performance. Not a house of commerce. Prayer is not a segment of church life—it is the lifeblood. Without it, the house is empty, the power is missing, and the glory departs.

Real prayer births things that cannot be fabricated. It creates openings in the unseen realm. It silences demonic strategies before they manifest. It unlocks resources, softens hardened hearts, exposes lies, and aligns the believer with the divine agenda. But it must be sustained. This is where many falter. They begin in passion but end in fatigue. They pray until it is inconvenient. They war until the answers delay. But glory demands endurance.

Daniel prayed faithfully three times a day, even when a decree threatened his life. His commitment was not a stunt— it was a lifestyle. And because of it, lions could not consume him. When he sought understanding through fasting and prayer, the answer was dispatched immediately—but delayed twenty-one days due to demonic resistance (Daniel 10:12–13). Yet Daniel did not stop. He prayed until the answer arrived. Not because he doubted, but because he knew something was shifting in the unseen.

This is the nature of warfare prayer. It is not always instant. It contends. It tears down strongholds. It fights fatigue, silence, and delay. It resists resignation. It says, "Even if I see nothing, I know something is happening." That kind of faith attracts glory. Because it believes God is faithful even when visible evidence is lacking.

Prayer that shifts things is often birthed in secret. Jesus instructed, "When you pray, go into your room and shut the door" (Matthew 6:6). Hidden places carry weight. What is prayed in secret is rewarded in public. The most powerful moments of spiritual release often trace their origins to unseen hours on bare floors, tear-soaked pillows, and whispered groans no one else hears. But God hears. And He remembers.

One of the clearest modern examples of this is the prayer movement that birthed revival on the island of Fiji. In the late 1990s, intercessors across villages began to fast and pray in unity for national repentance. Corruption, crime, and division plagued the land. But as prayer intensified, reports emerged of rivers healing, dead reefs reviving, and entire villages reconciling. Scientific experts could not explain it. But the Church knew: something had shifted. Glory had returned. And it started with prayer.

This is the invitation for every believer. Not to become eloquent, but to become engaged. Not to impress, but to intercede. Prayer is not reserved for the "prayer warriors." It is the breath of the believer. Without it, spiritual life withers. With it, the heavens open. Glory descends.

But glory-prayer requires honesty. It does not mask pain. It does not recite rehearsed lines. It groans when words fail. Romans 8:26 tells us that the Spirit helps in our weakness, interceding with groanings too deep for words. This is not poetic exaggeration. It is reality. The Holy Spirit takes hold of our burdens and gives them language. When we cannot articulate the ache, He does.

And the Father listens. He bends near. Not to analyze, but to respond. Prayer does not change God—but it gives Him room to change us and move through us. It is not about volume. It is about surrender. Some of the most powerful prayers are whispered through tears: "Lord, help me." "Lord, heal them." "Lord, do not pass me by."

Persistence in prayer is not stubbornness. It is alignment. It keeps knocking until the door opens—not because God is withholding, but because the process prepares us to steward what we are asking for. The delay refines our motives. The repetition sharpens our ears. The waiting matures our faith. And when the answer comes, it rests on ground that has been tilled by prayer.

Prayer until something shifts does not mean demanding your way. It means yielding to His way. Jesus, in the garden of Gethsemane, prayed in agony. Blood mingled with sweat. Three times He asked if the cup could pass. But He ended with, "Not My will, but Yours be done" (Luke 22:42). That was not defeat—it was surrender. And through that surrender, glory broke through. The cross became the gateway to resurrection. The agony produced access. And it was prayer that held the door open.

There is a price to this kind of praying. It will cost sleep. It will cost reputation. It will cost comfort. But what it produces cannot be gained any other way. The soul that has travailed in prayer carries something sacred. A weight. A fragrance. A spiritual authority that no title can match. Glory does not fall on the casual. It rests on those who have paid the price in the secret place.

Churches can be built with programs, but they are sustained by prayer. Families can survive through effort, but they thrive through intercession. Ministries can grow through charisma, but they endure through consecration. If glory is to return to our homes, pulpits, and communities, it must come through people who refuse to stop praying when it gets hard.

You may not see it yet, but something is shifting. Every prayer is a seed. Every tear is a cry that echoes in heaven. Every groan is a note in a symphony that heaven hears clearly. Keep praying. Keep pressing. Keep knocking. You are not wasting words—you are releasing glory.

Do not grow weary. Do not measure effectiveness by immediate results. Glory does not follow formulas. It follows faith. And faith keeps praying until something shifts. Something moves. Something breaks. Something opens.

Pray like Moses, who stood between judgment and mercy. Pray like Elijah, who birthed rain through intercession. Pray like Anna, who spent decades in the temple waiting for the

Messiah. Pray like Jesus, who retreated often to lonely places—not to escape, but to commune.

Pray until your mind aligns. Until your flesh yields. Until your spirit rises. Until your atmosphere changes. Until your children return. Until the chains break. Until the fire falls.

Pray until something shifts.

Chapter 10: Worship That Draws Heaven Down

Worship is not a performance. It is not a warm-up for preaching, nor a musical interlude between church announcements and the sermon. Worship is warfare. It is intimacy. It is surrender. And more than anything else, worship is the atmosphere that draws heaven to earth. It creates a landing place for the glory of God—not because God is drawn to sound, but because He is drawn to spirit and truth.

When Jesus spoke to the Samaritan woman at the well, He dismantled centuries of religious debate in a single sentence: "The hour is coming, and is now here, when the true worshipers will worship the Father in spirit and truth" (John 4:23). He was not suggesting a new musical trend. He was pointing to the posture of the heart that attracts the presence of God. Worship that draws heaven down is not confined by location, tempo, or instrumentation. It is marked by authenticity, purity, and reverence.

God has always responded to worship. Not because He needs it, but because it is the rightful response to who He is. In the days of the tabernacle, the Levites ministered before the Lord with songs and instruments—not for entertainment, but for encounter. When Solomon dedicated the temple, the priests and singers were united in praise. As they lifted their voices, the glory of God filled the house to such an extent that the priests could not stand to minister (2 Chronicles 5:13–14). The cloud of His presence descended, not in response to sacrifice alone, but to worship.

The pattern has not changed. Where God is exalted with purity, humility, and awe, His glory rests. Worship is not about us. It is not driven by preference, mood, or style. It is not meant to reflect culture—it is meant to reflect heaven. True worship dethrones the self and enthrones the Savior. It pulls the heart away from distractions and centers it on the worthiness of God.

The word "worship" in Scripture is derived from the Old English *worth-ship*—the act of declaring the worth of someone. It is also rooted in the Hebrew word *shachah*, meaning "to bow down." That image is not accidental. Worship is not a casual activity—it is a posture of surrender. It is the recognition that God is holy, other, majestic, and altogether beyond comparison. And yet, in worship, that same God draws near.

In Acts 16, Paul and Silas found themselves in the innermost prison, their backs torn by stripes, their feet fastened in stocks. No crowd. No comfort. But at midnight, they sang. They worshiped. Not because of their condition, but in spite of it. And heaven responded. The earth shook. Chains fell off. Doors opened. Worship in the dark released divine intervention. That is the power of spirit-born praise—it invites the supernatural into the natural.

This kind of worship is rare because it is costly. It does not come from convenience. It rises from conviction. It is Job, scraping his wounds, saying, "Though He slay me, I will hope in Him" (Job 13:15). It is David, whose child has died, going into the house of the Lord to worship (2 Samuel 12:20). It is Habakkuk, standing in famine, declaring, "Yet I will rejoice in the Lord" (Habakkuk 3:18). Worship in pain is not denial—it is defiance. It tells the darkness that it cannot mute the song.

Worship draws heaven down not just because it exalts God, but because it humbles man. It breaks pride. It melts pretense. It lifts the soul above fear, confusion, and shame. It aligns the heart with eternal reality. And when that alignment happens, glory descends. Not always with shaking and fire— but with weight, with stillness, with undeniable presence.

Throughout history, revivals have always been preceded and sustained by worship. During the Welsh Revival of 1904, churches overflowed not just with preaching, but with spontaneous praise. Men wept in the streets. Coal miners sang hymns underground. There were no microphones, no schedules. Worship erupted, and the glory fell. Bars closed. Crime plummeted. Because when heaven invades, everything changes.

The same is true today. In places where believers gather to exalt God with undivided hearts, the glory comes. Not always visibly, but unmistakably. Tears fall. Conviction pierces. Joy rises. Healing flows. Worship is not emotionalism—it is spiritual alignment. And aligned hearts create holy ground.

But worship must be guarded. In many places, it has become performance-driven. Stage lights, polished sets, and rehearsed songs have replaced the raw hunger for God. The danger is not in excellence, but in emptiness. When the heart is disengaged, the song is hollow. When applause is the goal, glory departs. The presence of God cannot be manipulated. It comes where He is honored.

Isaiah saw the Lord high and lifted up, and the train of His robe filled the temple. Seraphim cried out, "Holy, holy, holy is the Lord of hosts; the whole earth is full of His glory" (Isaiah 6:3). That is worship in its purest form: declaring who God is until the atmosphere is saturated with His reality. And Isaiah's response was not applause—it was repentance. "Woe is me!" he cried. Worship exposes. It cleanses. It commissions.

The reason many do not carry glory is because they have not yet embraced worship as a lifestyle. It is not confined to Sundays. It is not limited to songs. Worship is obedience. It is purity. It is thanksgiving in the mundane. When Abraham was called to offer Isaac, he told his servants, "I and the boy will go over there and worship" (Genesis 22:5). He did not say, "We will sing." He said, "We will worship." For him, worship was obedience in sacrifice. That is what draws heaven down—hearts that obey even when it costs.

In Luke 7, a sinful woman broke an alabaster jar and poured it on Jesus' feet. She wept, kissed His feet, and wiped them with her hair. Others criticized. But Jesus said, "She has done a beautiful thing to Me." Her worship was extravagant because her revelation was deep. She knew she had been forgiven much, and so she loved much. That love became worship. And the fragrance filled the room.

True worship always costs something. Time. Pride. Reputation. But the fragrance of worship is what causes heaven to linger. God does not seek singers. He seeks worshipers—those who worship in spirit and in truth. Not perfect, but honest. Not flawless, but surrendered. Glory is not found in performance—it is found in pursuit.

Leonard Ravenhill once said, "Entertainment is the devil's substitute for joy. The more joy you have in the Lord, the less entertainment you need." This is why so much of modern worship falls flat—it seeks to entertain instead of enthrone. But the Church must return to the altar. To the posture of Mary at Jesus' feet. To the incense of surrendered lives.

Worship that draws heaven down is often birthed in silence. In moments when the song fades and the soul waits. It is Elijah on the mountain, hearing God not in the wind or fire, but in the whisper (1 Kngs 19:12). Worship makes space for the whisper. It listens. It waits. It trembles. And when the whisper comes, so does the glory.

This kind of worship cannot be rushed. It cannot be faked. It requires stillness. Reverence. Focus. It is not passive—it is powerful. It reshapes hearts. It realigns priorities. It releases revelation. It prepares the vessel for divine visitation.

If you want to carry glory, you must become a worshiper. Not just in song, but in spirit. Not just with lips, but with life. When you rise in the morning, worship. When you face conflict, worship. When you feel dry, worship. When breakthrough comes, worship. Let your life become a continuous offering— a living sacrifice, holy and acceptable to God.

Worship is the highway of glory. It is the place where earth meets heaven and man meets God. It is where burdens fall, fear dissolves, and identity is restored. And it is available— right now, wherever you are. You do not need a platform. You need a heart postured low and a spirit turned upward.

Lift your voice. Bow your heart. Silence the noise. Lift your eyes. And let the glory fall.

Chapter 11: Obedience Is Better Than Sacrifice

God is not impressed by what we lay on the altar if our hearts refuse to follow Him off it. He is not moved by offerings that mask rebellion. He is not flattered by spiritual activity that lacks submission. To carry His glory, one must walk in His ways. It is obedience—not talent, ambition, or sacrifice—that attracts the weight of His presence. As Samuel told Saul with piercing clarity, "To obey is better than sacrifice, and to listen than the fat of rams" (1 Samuel 15:22). God values surrendered will more than spectacular gestures.

Obedience is the divine language of trust. It is the tangible proof of love. Jesus said, "If you love Me, you will keep My commandments" (John 14:15). He did not say, "Sing about Me." He did not say, "Give to Me." He said, "Obey Me." The mark of intimacy is not how loudly we proclaim His name, but how fully we align with His voice. Glory rests where there is alignment. Where there is resistance, it withdraws.

Saul's downfall was not rooted in immorality, but in partial obedience. He was instructed to completely destroy the Amalekites and everything associated with them. Instead, he spared the king and kept the best livestock. When confronted, he claimed it was for sacrifice. He spiritualized his disobedience. But God was not fooled. The prophet's words still thunder through time: "Because you have rejected the word of the Lord, He has also rejected you" (1 Samuel 15:23). Glory does not rest on compromise.

Obedience is costly. It will often require what logic rejects. When God told Noah to build an ark, there was no rain in sight. When He told Abraham to leave his country, no destination was named. When He told Joshua to march around Jericho, military wisdom was nowhere to be found. Yet in every case, glory followed obedience. The flood came, and Noah was safe. The journey began, and Abraham became the father of nations. The walls fell, and Israel took the land. God's glory is not limited by human understanding—but it is released through human obedience.

There is a subtle deception that whispers, "As long as my heart is sincere, my actions do not matter." But Scripture dismantles that lie. Nadab and Abihu, sons of Aaron, offered unauthorized fire before the Lord—something He had not commanded. And fire came out from His presence and consumed them (Leviticus 10:1–2). They were not pagans. They were priests. But zeal without obedience is dangerous. Glory does not rest on assumption. It rests on precision.

Jesus modeled obedience to the point of death. "He humbled Himself by becoming obedient to the point of death, even death on a cross" (Philippians 2:8). His miracles were not random—they were responses to the Father's leading. He said, "I do nothing on My own authority, but speak just as the Father taught Me" (John 8:28). This is why the Spirit descended and remained upon Him. He was not just anointed—He was aligned.

The greatest outpourings of glory in history have come through people who obeyed in secret before they were used in public. Corrie ten Boom hid Jews during the Holocaust, risking her life daily. When captured and imprisoned, she continued to serve, preach, and forgive. The presence of God followed her because her life was a continual "yes" to the will of God. Not a loud one. Not always a joyful one. But a faithful one.

Obedience does not always look dramatic. Sometimes it looks like forgiving when you would rather remain bitter. Sometimes it means staying when you want to leave—or leaving when you want to stay. Sometimes it means apologizing first. Declining the platform. Refusing the shortcut. Turning the other cheek. Closing your mouth. Changing your plans. Canceling the trip. Returning the tithe. Waking up early. Going to bed without answers. Laying your Isaac on the altar. And walking back down the mountain alone.

It is in these small, hidden obediences that glory takes root. Heaven watches how we respond when no one else sees. When the applause is gone. When the assignment hurts. When we are tired, overlooked, and misunderstood. Obedience in the shadows builds authority in the light.

Jesus said the wise man hears His words and does them. The foolish man hears and does not act. Both hear. But only one obeys. And the difference is seen when storms come. One house stands. The other falls. Glory cannot rest where obedience is optional. It requires a foundation.

The reason obedience is so powerful is because it dethrones self. It confronts pride. It demands surrender. Obedience says, "Your will, not mine." It is what took Jesus from Gethsemane to Golgotha. It is what makes intercession effectual. What makes preaching powerful. What makes worship real. Obedience gives weight to everything else. Without it, sacrifice becomes noise. Ministry becomes performance. Faith becomes fantasy.

One of the most sobering examples in Scripture is Uzzah. When David brought the Ark of the Covenant back to Jerusalem, they placed it on a cart—a method God had not prescribed. When the oxen stumbled, Uzzah reached out to steady it. And he died. Instantly. It seems harsh. But God had made it clear: the Ark must be carried on the shoulders of consecrated priests (1 Chronicles 15:13–15). They had disobeyed. And even a well-meaning hand could not fix what only obedience could correct.

David later acknowledged the mistake and made the necessary changes. This time, the Levites carried the Ark properly. Sacrifices were offered. Worship erupted. And the glory returned. This is the grace of God: obedience, once restored, opens the door for glory to come again.

Obedience is not always about instruction—it is also about timing. The children of Israel were told to enter the Promised Land. They refused, afraid of giants. When God rebuked them, they suddenly changed their minds and attempted to go. But it was too late. Moses warned them not to move forward, but they went anyway. They were defeated.

Because delayed obedience, disguised as repentance, is still disobedience (Numbers 14:40–45).

To carry glory, we must move when He moves. We must stop when He stops. The cloud by day and fire by night were not symbols—they were signals. The people moved only when the presence moved. This is worship in action: obeying His direction, not just admiring His beauty.

Obedience releases joy. It does not imprison—it frees. When we obey, we are no longer slaves to self, to fear, to opinion. We are sons and daughters, led by the Spirit, anchored in truth. We stop striving to prove ourselves. We stop performing for approval. We simply follow. And in that following, we are transformed.

Glory changes environments. Obedience changes people. And when the two converge, revival becomes more than a hope—it becomes a reality. Not because a man preached well, or a song was sung with emotion, but because hearts bowed to the King. In homes. In secret places. In ordinary days filled with holy yeses.

If the Church is to host the glory of God in this generation, it must return to obedience. Not legalism. Not lifeless rules. But love-driven surrender. The kind that says yes before the question is even asked. The kind that follows even when it does not understand. The kind that stays tender in a hard world.

There is a remnant rising—people who will not just talk about God's will, but do it. Who will forgive seventy times seven.

Who will honor when it is not returned. Who will stay when others walk away. Who will lay hands on the sick, share with the poor, guard their tongues, walk in purity, seek justice, and love mercy. Not for recognition. Not for applause. But because they know that obedience attracts the presence. And presence is the reward.

Heaven is not searching for talent. It is not impressed by resumes. It looks for hearts that tremble at God's word. For lives that bend when He speaks. For vessels that move when He says move—and wait when He says wait. These are the ones who will carry the weight. These are the ones who will walk in glory.

You may never preach to crowds. You may never write books, lead worship, or build platforms. But if you obey—quietly, consistently, joyfully—heaven will rest on you. The glory will not be loud, but it will be heavy. People will sense peace when you enter. Light when you speak. Fire when you pray. Because God walks with those who obey.

You cannot buy glory. You cannot fake it. You can only host it. And hosting it begins with obedience.

Not someday. Not later. Now.

Chapter 12: Repentance as a Glory Gateway

There is a sound that moves heaven. It is not always loud. It does not originate from a stage or fill an auditorium. It rises quietly from the soul that is broken over sin and desperate for restoration. It is the sound of repentance. And where that sound is heard, glory follows. Not because repentance is emotional—but because it is the alignment that makes room for God to dwell again. Repentance is not just a step on the way to revival—it is the door through which the glory enters.

In a world increasingly numb to conviction and allergic to correction, the message of repentance feels offensive. But to heaven, repentance is beautiful. It is the song of return. It is the turning of the heart back to its Creator. Without it, there is no cleansing. Without it, there is no intimacy. Without it, there is no glory.

The prophet Isaiah had a vision that would shake any soul. He saw the Lord high and lifted up, with seraphim declaring "Holy, holy, holy." The temple shook. The threshold trembled. Smoke filled the space. And Isaiah's first response was not awe—it was anguish. "Woe is me!" he cried, "For I am lost; for I am a man of unclean lips" (Isaiah 6:5). That was repentance. Not manufactured sorrow. Not forced humility. It was the collision of flesh and glory. And it produced transformation.

Then came the coal. Taken from the altar and placed on his lips. Cleansing. Consecration. Commissioning. But the fire did not fall until repentance rose. Glory came because Isaiah did not excuse his condition. He confessed it. He did not hide. He did not rationalize. He repented.

This pattern continues throughout Scripture. David, after his affair with Bathsheba and the murder of her husband, did not write a defense. He wrote Psalm 51—a raw, vulnerable plea for mercy. "Create in me a clean heart, O God," he cried, "and renew a right spirit within me... Do not cast me away from Your presence, and do not take Your Holy Spirit from me" (Psalm 51:10–11). David understood what many forget: unrepented sin may not remove salvation, but it can grieve the Spirit and drive away the glory.

Repentance is not about shame. It is about restoration. It is not a punishment—it is a pathway. It says, "I want to be close again. I want to be clean again. I want to be whole again." And God responds. Always. He is not looking for flawless performance—He is looking for brokenness that bends back toward Him. "The sacrifices of God are a broken spirit; a broken and contrite heart, O God, You will not despise" (Psalm 51:17).

When Peter denied Jesus three times, he was crushed. The rooster crowed, and the look from Jesus pierced him. He wept bitterly—not from embarrassment, but from conviction. And later, on a Galilean shoreline, Jesus restored him. Not through shame, but through questions: "Do you love Me?" With each answer, Jesus reaffirmed his calling. But the turning point came at repentance. Without it, Peter would have remained locked in regret. With it, he stepped into glory. Preaching on the day of Pentecost. Healing the sick. Raising the dead. Proclaiming Christ with boldness.

Repentance does not shrink a person—it refines them. It restores authority. It clears the atmosphere. It makes room for the Spirit to move without hindrance. Unconfessed sin is not a private issue. It blocks rivers. It dulls discernment. It closes the heavens. But repentance reopens the flow.

When revival swept through the Hebrides Islands in 1949, it was not because of a preacher or a program. It was because of a small group of intercessors who got honest. They read Psalm 24 aloud—"Who shall ascend the hill of the Lord? He who has clean hands and a pure heart." They wept. They repented. They confessed their compromise. And glory came. People were saved without sermons. Conviction fell without invitations. The fear of the Lord returned. Because repentance had prepared the ground.

There is a difference between remorse and repentance. Remorse feels sorry. Repentance turns. Remorse feels shame. Repentance surrenders. Judas felt remorse. He returned the silver. But he did not return to the Savior. Peter repented—and was restored. This distinction is crucial. God does not despise those who fall. He draws near to those who admit they have.

The modern Church has, at times, neglected this truth. We offer comfort but avoid confrontation. We promise peace without purity. We celebrate growth without addressing sin.

And in doing so, we build large rooms with no weight. No glory. No presence. Because God does not dwell where sin is excused. He dwells where sin is confessed.

Even in the book of Acts, when revival was at its height, Peter's message was not seeker-friendly. He declared the guilt of the people and called them to repentance. "Repent therefore, and turn back, that your sins may be blotted out, that times of refreshing may come from the presence of the Lord" (Acts 3:19). Repentance leads to refreshing. Glory is not the reward of spiritual charisma. It is the result of holy surrender.

This is true in homes, not just churches. Marriages are restored when repentance enters the conversation. Children return when parents humble themselves. Bitterness breaks when the offended repents for how they handled the offense. Even in private prayer, breakthrough happens when we stop just asking and start confessing.

One of the hidden beauties of repentance is that it creates intimacy. Sin separates. Even if God's love remains, the nearness fades. Repentance closes the gap. It says, "God, I want nothing between us." And He rushes in. The prodigal son, rehearsing his apology, was met by a Father running to embrace him. There was no long speech. Just repentance— and restoration. The ring. The robe. The celebration. Not because the son was worthy, but because the father was waiting.

The enemy fears repentance because it disarms him. He thrives in hiddenness. He manipulates guilt into silence. But repentance brings everything into the light. And in the light, darkness dies. There is no condemnation in Christ—but there is conviction. And that conviction is a gift. It is the gentle hand of the Spirit pointing the soul back to the place of glory.

Even nations are transformed through repentance. Nineveh was a wicked city. Violent. Corrupt. Idolatrous. But when Jonah preached, the king responded. He called for a fast. He dressed in sackcloth. He led the people in repentance. And God relented from judgment. Revival visited Nineveh—not because of theology, but because of repentance. This principle has not expired. Where sin is confessed, mercy flows.

The pathway to personal glory is not found in striving. It is found in surrender. The glory of God does not fall on proud hearts. It falls on broken ones. And every crack becomes a place where light enters. Repentance is not a one-time event. It is a lifestyle. Not because God demands groveling, but because the closer you get to the light, the more you see what still needs cleansing.

Paul, near the end of his life, called himself the chief of sinners—not as false humility, but as one deeply aware of his continual need for grace. This awareness did not disqualify him. It prepared him to carry greater glory. Because God resists the proud but gives grace to the humble.

Glory is not maintained by perfection. It is maintained by repentance. The vessel that knows how to return quickly will never run dry. The heart that says, "Search me, O God, and know my heart," will never grow cold (Psalm 139:23). Repentance keeps the fire burning.

In the days of Josiah, a young king rediscovered the Book of the Law in the ruins of the temple. When it was read aloud, he tore his robes and wept. He called the nation to repentance. Altars to Baal were torn down. Idols were destroyed. Worship was restored. And Scripture says, "Before him there was no king like him, who turned to the Lord with all his heart... nor did any like him arise after him" (2 Kings 23:25). His reign was marked by repentance—and it released national renewal.

This is the cry for today. A Church unashamed of the altar. A generation that repents quickly. Leaders who confess before being exposed. Homes that choose purity over pride. Cities that cry out for mercy. Repentance is not the path to shame. It is the path to glory.

If you want to carry His presence, you must carry His heart. And His heart is holy. There is no room for casual compromise. There is no glory without cleansing. But the cleansing is not impossible. It is a prayer away. One whispered admission. One honest cry. One turning of the heart—and the glory returns.

Do not wait. Do not hide. Do not run. Bring it to the altar. Lay it down. Speak it aloud. Let Him wash you. Let Him fill you. Let Him rest on you again. The greatest glory is not in never falling—it is in returning quickly. And every time you do, He receives you. Not with condemnation—but with fire.

Repentance is the gateway. The glory is waiting.

Chapter 13: Holiness Makes You Heavy

There is a difference between being gifted and being weighty. Gifting impresses, but it is holiness that gives spiritual gravity. The world applauds charisma, but heaven honors consecration. To carry the weight of God's glory, one must first carry the weight of His holiness. Not the superficial kind rooted in appearances, but the sacred fire that comes from walking in clean hands and pure hearts. Holiness is not a legalistic concept—it is a divine atmosphere. And when a person lives in it, they become heavy with God.

Holiness is not the absence of mistakes; it is the presence of God. It is the separation from anything that contaminates intimacy. It is not about rigid rule-keeping, but about radical alignment. When the Israelites beheld Mount Sinai, it was not merely the fire and smoke that terrified them—it was the holiness. The mountain shook, not because of drama, but because of presence. Holiness is what makes God unlike any other. It is the very nature of His being. And to walk with Him closely, we must walk in it too.

When Uzziah became king of Judah, he began well. He sought God in the days of Zechariah and prospered. But when he became strong, pride filled his heart. He entered the temple to offer incense—something only the priests were allowed to do. Azariah the priest and eighty others confronted him. But Uzziah, enraged, refused to back down. And at that moment, leprosy broke out on his forehead. He was driven out of the house of the Lord and remained a leper until the day he died (2 Chronicles 26:16–21). What began in power ended in disgrace. Not because of failure in gifting—but because of a breach in holiness.

God's glory rests on those who fear Him. Holiness is the foundation of that fear. Not terror—but reverence. Not distance—but awe. It is the quiet knowing that He is God and we are not. It is the joyful awareness that He dwells in purity and invites us into it. When that awareness becomes our reality, our lives begin to carry spiritual weight. Our prayers pierce darkness. Our words carry fire. Our presence changes rooms—not because of us, but because of Him in us.

One of the most powerful revivals in recorded history took place in Pyongyang, Korea, in 1907—long before the nation was divided. During a Bible conference, the Spirit of conviction fell. A missionary named Dr. Howard Moffett described what happened: Korean pastors began confessing sins aloud in front of each other. Not vague, general confessions, but specific, heart-wrenching admissions. Hidden offenses. Bitterness. Jealousy. Theft. Immorality. The holiness of God had entered the room, and no one could pretend. The revival that followed swept across the region, and hundreds of churches were planted. It was not the result of great preaching. It was the result of great cleansing. Holiness made the people heavy.

In Isaiah's vision, the angels did not cry, "Love, love, love" or "Power, power, power." They cried, "Holy, holy, holy is the

Lord of hosts; the whole earth is full of His glory" (Isaiah 6:3). The link between holiness and glory is unmistakable. You cannot host the weight of His presence while entertaining what grieves Him. Glory rests where purity dwells.

The Apostle Peter exhorted the early Church, "As He who called you is holy, you also be holy in all your conduct" (1 Peter 1:15). This was not optional. It was not cultural. It was eternal. Holiness was not reserved for priests—it was required of every believer who desired nearness. The early Church carried such weight because it lived set apart. When Ananias and Saophira lied about their offering, they fell dead in the presence of God (Acts 5). That was not legalism. That was the result of holiness in the room.

To be holy means to be other. To be separate. Not isolated from people, but from sin. It means our entertainment changes. Our speech changes. Our desires change. Not because we are better—but because we are burning. Holiness is the inner fire that refuses to let compromise settle. It convicts. It cleanses. It calls us higher.

During the Welsh Revival of 1904, Evan Roberts, a young man with no formal theological training, became a catalyst for one of the most profound spiritual awakenings in Europe. What marked the revival was not sensationalism—but holiness. Meetings would begin with silence and end with repentance. People would confess sin spontaneously. Taverns emptied. Crime rates plummeted. Judges were left with no cases. The presence was so thick that people felt it in the streets. All because hearts were clean. Holiness gave them weight.

Many want the manifestation without the consecration. But the glory of God cannot rest on what resists refinement. The fire of God is both purifying and empowering. You cannot carry it without being consumed. John the Baptist declared that Jesus would baptize "with the Holy Spirit and fire" (Matthew 3:11). That fire burns away the excess, the idols, the pride, the bitterness, the impurity. It does not destroy us—it makes us carriers.

Holiness is not self-righteousness. It does not parade spiritual performance. It does not look down on others. True holiness makes you humble. It makes you gentle. It makes you burn with compassion. Jesus was the holiest man to ever walk the earth—and He was also the most approachable. Sinners ran to Him. The broken touched Him. The unclean wept at His feet. His holiness did not repel them—it drew them. Because it was real. And it carried weight.

There is a generation rising that is tired of performance. Tired of church without change. Tired of words without wonder. They are not looking for more entertainment. They are looking for weight. For presence. For fire. And that weight will only come when the altars are restored—not physical altars, but the altar of the heart. Where pride is laid down. Where sin is confessed. Where lives are surrendered again.

The Church does not need more innovation. It needs more consecration. Glory is not a result of programs. It is the fruit of purity. When hearts are holy, heaven responds. When motives are clean, miracles return. When the fear of the Lord returns, the power of the Lord will not be far behind.

Holiness begins in the secret place. It is forged in private decisions. What you choose when no one sees. What you watch when no one knows. What you say when no one hears. That is where weight is built. Glory does not rest on talent—it rests on trust. And God trusts the holy.

There was a man named B.H. Clendennen, a humble preacher who planted Bible schools and raised up evangelists all over the world. Those who encountered him often described a tangible sense of the fear of the Lord surrounding him. He was not famous in popular culture, but his life carried weight. He prayed more than he spoke. He wept over souls. He lived clean. And wherever he went, glory followed. Because holiness had made him heavy.

This is what the Lord is calling His people back to—not performance, but presence. Not busyness, but burning. Not influence, but intimacy. You do not have to be perfect to be holy. But you do have to be willing. Willing to let the Spirit convict you. Willing to let the Word correct you. Willing to walk away from what grieves Him. Willing to choose the narrow road when the broad path is easier.

He is looking for those who will say, "Here I am, Lord. Cleanse me. Use me. Make me holy." And when He finds that heart, He fills it with glory. That is what happened with Daniel. Though surrounded by paganism, he remained undefiled. He fasted. He prayed. He refused to compromise. And God gave him visions, wisdom, favor, and protection. Even lions could not devour what holiness had covered.

To be holy is to be usable. God does not anoint vessels that remain dirty. He cleanses them first. Paul wrote, "Therefore, if anyone cleanses himself from what is dishonorable, he will be a vessel for honorable use, set apart as holy... ready for every good work" (2 Timothy 2:21). Holiness makes you ready. Ready for power. Ready for purpose. Ready for glory.

The cost of holiness is high. You will be misunderstood. Mocked. Sometimes alone. But you will never be empty. The weight of God's presence will rest on you. People may not understand it—but they will feel it. They may not like it—but they will respect it. Because holiness leaves a mark. It lingers in a room long after you have left.

This is what made Jesus unstoppable. He walked in perfect holiness. The demons trembled. The sick were healed. The dead were raised. Not just because He was the Son of God— but because He was holy. And He has called us to follow Him. Not in performance—but in purity. Not in image—but in substance.

If we want the glory to return, holiness must lead the way. Not as a doctrine—but as a lifestyle. Not out of fear—but out of love. He is holy. And when we walk in holiness, we walk with Him.

And when we walk with Him, we carry the weight.

Chapter 14: The Anonymity of Glory

There is a way God works that is not loud. It does not demand attention, nor does it crave recognition. It flows in silence, moves in humility, and settles where the crowd is not looking. It is the way of glory veiled in anonymity. This kind of glory does not exalt the vessel—it exalts the Presence. It does not seek platforms or applause. It hides in the secret, the ordinary, the overlooked. And yet, it changes everything.

When the glory of God rests upon a life, the temptation is to announce it. To let others know that heaven has touched you. But glory is not proven by visibility. It is proven by weight. Some of the heaviest vessels are hidden. Some of the most powerful ministries remain unnamed. Because the glory of God prefers the humble. It chooses the low places. The secret places. The quiet places.

God revealed this truth in Bethlehem. When the King of all creation stepped into time, He did not come with armies. He came as an infant. Wrapped in cloth. Laid in a feeding trough. Born to a virgin who was barely known. The Word became flesh, and the world barely noticed. But glory was there. Heaven's light in the smallest place. The most important moment in human history was cloaked in silence. Because glory does not always come with volume. Sometimes, it comes veiled.

Moses did not begin with a burning bush. He began with forty years of anonymity. A prince turned fugitive, forgotten on the backside of the desert. He tended sheep that were not even his. No one called his name. No one remembered his past. No one saw his preparation. But God did. And in that wilderness, away from the noise, glory met him. The bush burned with fire but was not consumed. And the voice of the Lord called out—not in the palace, but in obscurity. Because God often chooses the hidden places to release His holiest moments.

Anonymity is not punishment. It is preparation. It strips the soul of performance. It tests motives. It refines desires. It reveals whether we want to carry God's presence or just be seen. It is in the hidden years that weight is built. God is not impressed by quick ascents. He is drawn to deep roots. When no one is watching, will you still pray? When no one notices, will you still fast? When there is no stage, will you still worship? These are the questions that anonymity answers. And when the answers are yes, glory follows.

Jesus spent thirty years in anonymity. No miracles. No sermons. No crowds. Just carpentry, obedience, silence. The Son of God learned obedience through what He suffered. Not in public, but in private. And when the time came, He stepped into ministry not as a celebrity, but as a servant. And the Father's voice echoed from heaven, "This is My beloved Son, in whom I am well pleased" (Matthew 3:17). He had not yet healed the sick or raised the dead. But the Father was pleased. Not with performance—but with surrender.

In Luke 24, after the resurrection, Jesus walked with two disciples on the road to Emmaus. But they did not recognize Him. He opened the Scriptures to them. He walked with them. He ate with them. Only when He broke the bread did their eyes open. And then He vanished. Glory had walked beside them in complete anonymity. No grand display. No spotlight. Just Presence. Quiet. Patient. Transforming.

The prophet Elijah was known for fire. He called it down from heaven on Mount Carmel. He confronted kings. He stopped the rain. But when he fled to the wilderness in despair, God met him—not in the wind, not in the earthquake, not in the fire, but in a still small voice (1 Kings 19:12). Glory whispered. Because God was teaching him that His greatest presence is not always loud. Sometimes it is hidden. Sometimes it is gentle. But it is no less powerful.

There is a danger in seeking visibility instead of weight. The enemy does not mind fame if it comes without fire. He does not fear popularity that lacks purity. But he trembles before those who walk with God in the secret place. Because they carry something he cannot imitate. Something born in silence. Something birthed in prayer. Something forged in anonymity.

When revival came to the Indonesian island of Timor in the 1960s, it did not begin with famous preachers. It began with a small group of believers who gave themselves to fasting and prayer. The stories that emerged were startling. The dead raised. The sick healed. Demons cast out. Whole villages turned to Christ. But the vessels God used were unknown. No one sought a name. They sought His face. And the glory came.

John the Baptist was a voice crying in the wilderness. He had no fancy robes. No temple access. But he carried weight. He prepared the way for Jesus without ever performing a miracle. And when his disciples were concerned about Jesus gaining more followers, John responded, "He must increase, but I must decrease" (John 3:30). That is the posture of those who carry glory. They point away from themselves. They make room for the King.

Paul, the apostle to the Gentiles, wrote letters that shook empires. But much of his life was spent in prisons, deserts, and shipwrecks. He was rejected, beaten, stoned, and forgotten. He was not admired by crowds. He was not celebrated by the powerful. Yet his life carried weight because he lived for the audience of One. He said, "I count all things as loss for the surpassing worth of knowing Christ" (Philippians 3:8). That kind of knowing cannot be bought. It is forged in the fire of hiddenness.

Anonymity is not the absence of calling. It is the cocoon of calling. It is the place where God prepares you without fanfare. Where He tests the vessel before filling it with glory. Many want the oil, but few are willing to be crushed. Many want the fire, but few are willing to be refined. But the hidden ones know the price. They are not seeking a platform—they are becoming one for God to stand on.

When God wanted to redeem humanity, He did not send an army. He sent a baby. When He wanted to speak to Samuel,

95

He did not shout. He whispered in the night. When He wanted to anoint a king, He bypassed seven older brothers and chose the shepherd boy in the field. Because God sees differently. He does not look at appearance. He looks at the heart. And He still does.

The most dangerous place for a person is not obscurity. It is visibility without maturity. Fame without formation. Exposure without sanctification. That is why God often hides those He plans to use. He keeps them close. He works on them in the dark. He allows misunderstandings, delays, closed doors—not to harm them, but to shape them. Because when they finally emerge, they will not be driven by ego. They will be driven by glory.

In China, the underground Church has grown exponentially. Believers gather in basements, forests, and secret homes. They have no microphones. No lights. No marketing teams. But they carry glory. Because they have learned to walk with God in the dark. And in the dark, they have discovered the light of His presence. Not as a theory—but as a flame.

This is the invitation: to embrace the hidden place. To welcome the anonymity that God uses to form His vessels. To choose depth over display. To choose intimacy over image. To be content to carry the fire, even when no one sees the flame. Because God sees. And in His time, He lifts. In His time, He reveals. But even if He never does, the weight of His presence is enough.

He is looking for those who will not trade consecration for clout. Who will not exchange holiness for hype. Who will not seek the approval of crowds at the expense of His voice. The anonymous glory carriers are rising. They do not need validation to burn. They are hidden, but they are holy. And heaven knows their names.

May we be counted among them. Not for recognition, but for revelation. Not to be known, but to make Him known. Not to build a brand, but to host His presence. That is the heart of a glory carrier.

Hidden, but burning.

Chapter 15: The Power of Silence and Solitude

God often speaks loudest when everything else is silent. The deep things of God are rarely discovered in noise, motion, or crowds. They are found in the stillness, in moments away from the eyes of others, in spaces so quiet they make the soul uncomfortable. Silence and solitude are not empty—they are full. They are not wasted time—they are sacred appointments. In a world that rewards noise and pace, these ancient rhythms have become rare. But those who carry God's glory understand their power. Because silence and solitude are where glory takes root.

Jesus understood this. Though constantly surrounded by multitudes, though healing, teaching, and working miracles, He made solitude His home. Mark writes, "Very early in the morning, while it was still dark, Jesus got up, left the house and went off to a solitary place, where He prayed" (Mark 1:35). This was not a one-time occurrence. It was His pattern. Before major decisions, after long days of ministry, at the height of popularity and even in deep grief, He withdrew. The Son of God—who had access to all power—chose silence and solitude again and again. Because glory thrives in stillness.

There is something about getting alone with God that exposes what we carry. In the silence, there are no masks. No performances. No distractions. Just you and the voice that formed you. And in that place, glory speaks. Not through thunder, but through whispers. Not in the earthquake, but in the gentle stillness. Elijah found this out after the showdown on Mount Carmel. After calling down fire, after defeating false prophets, he fled into the wilderness, overwhelmed and afraid. But when God came to meet him, He did not come with spectacle. He came with a still small voice (1 Kings 19:12). That voice changed Elijah more than fire ever could.

Solitude is not loneliness. It is intimacy. It is where God draws near to the willing. Throughout Scripture, He met His people in the wilderness—not to abandon them, but to reveal Himself. It was in the desert that Moses saw the burning bush. It was in isolation that Jacob wrestled with the angel. It was in exile that John received the Revelation. God's glory is not hindered by isolation. In fact, it often chooses it. Because there, the noise of the world fades and the soul can hear again.

In the 1600s, Brother Lawrence, a French lay brother in a Carmelite monastery, became known for his extraordinary awareness of God's presence. He worked in the kitchen, washing dishes and preparing meals. But it was in those mundane moments of silence that he cultivated constant communion with God. He wrote, "There is not in the world a kind of life more sweet and delightful than that of a continual conversation with God." He discovered what many miss: silence is not an absence—it is an invitation.

The world fears silence because it forces us to confront ourselves. In the quiet, our insecurities rise. Our fears speak louder. Our wounds become visible. But that is the place where healing begins. Because God does not heal what we hide. In silence, we bring our whole selves to Him—unfiltered, unguarded, undone. And He meets us there. Not to shame us, but to restore us. Silence creates space for transformation.

In 1904, Evan Roberts would spend hours in silence before God during the Welsh Revival. He would not rush into prayer. He would not immediately preach. He would wait. Sometimes, meetings would go on for hours before anyone said a word. People sat in holy awe, aware that God was present. And in that stillness, repentance would break out. Without prompting. Without pressure. Because the silence was not empty—it was filled with glory.

Solitude is not just a tool—it is a test. It tests whether God is enough. When there is no applause, no affirmation, no audience—will we still seek Him? Will we still show up? Will we still pray when no one sees? These are the questions that solitude answers. And those who answer them with yes become trustworthy with glory.

David learned this in the fields. Long before he faced Goliath, long before the songs and the throne, he was a shepherd. Alone with sheep. Alone with the stars. Alone with his harp. But he was not truly alone. In those silent nights, he learned the sound of God's voice. He wrote songs that still stir hearts. He cultivated boldness before he had an audience. And when the time came to stand before a giant, he did not waver. Because solitude had already made him strong.

The desert fathers of the early Church understood this well. Men like Anthony the Great left cities and comfort to seek God in the wilderness. Their lives were marked by discipline, silence, and prayer. They became spiritual giants—not through crowds, but through communion. Visitors would travel for days to spend a few moments in their presence. Because something tangible rested on them. Something weighty. Something born in the quiet. They carried glory.

Jesus told His disciples, "When you pray, go into your room, close the door and pray to your Father, who is unseen" (Matthew 6:6). The secret place is where public power is birthed. It is where motives are purified. Where burdens are lifted. Where intimacy is restored. The closed door is not a barrier—it is a passage. And those who pass through it discover a dimension of God that cannot be accessed in public.

Noise is the enemy of discernment. Many cannot hear God because they are too full of other voices. Social media, entertainment, endless opinions. But glory does not compete. It waits. It stands at the door and knocks. And it enters where it is welcomed. Silence is the sign that we are listening. It is the posture of reverence. It says, "Speak, Lord. Your servant is listening." And when we listen, He speaks.

In recent years, movements of silence and retreat have grown again. From monasteries to modern prayer rooms, people are rediscovering the sacredness of being still before God. No agenda. No noise. Just presence. And those who embrace this find that God is not distant. He has been waiting. Waiting for the world to slow down long enough to notice Him.

Charles Spurgeon, the great preacher, once said, "The best prayer often has more groans than words." Sometimes, the deepest communion with God happens without speech. It happens in tears. In stillness. In sighs too deep for words. Because the Spirit helps us in our weakness. And in that unspoken dialogue, we are changed.

Solitude is also where identity is affirmed. When Jesus was baptized, the Father declared, "This is my beloved Son, in whom I am well pleased" (Matthew 3:17). Immediately after, Jesus was led into the wilderness. Alone. Hungry. Tested. And yet, He stood firm. Because He had heard the voice. The solitude did not confuse Him—it confirmed Him. He knew who He was. And that clarity gave Him power.

In our generation, where visibility is currency and silence feels like loss, this chapter is a call to return. To find again the God who waits in the stillness. To build lives rooted not in noise, but in nearness. To walk away from the crowd long enough to hear heaven again.

Glory does not come to the distracted. It comes to the devoted. It comes to those who make space. Who slow down. Who listen. Who linger. The glory of God is not just an event—it is a habitation. And it begins with silence.

Some of the greatest intercessors who have shaped nations are unknown to the world. Elderly women praying in closets. Men who fast and weep in secret. Missionaries who pour out their hearts in silence before dawn. They may never trend. They may never publish. But heaven knows them. Because they have built a h story with God in the quiet. And their prayers echo in eternity.

This is what it means to be a glory carrier. Not just to display God, but to dwell with Him. Not just to speak of Him, but to sit with Him. And in that sitting, to become like Him. The quiet transforms us. It softens us. It strengthens us. It reveals the glory that words car not.

So close the door. Turn off the noise. Step into the silence. He is there.

Chapter 16: Brokenness Is the Road to Glory

The pathway to carrying the presence and power of God is not paved with ambition or adorned with applause. It is carved through brokenness. The kind of brokenness that strips pride, unmasks self-reliance, and humbles the soul before a holy God. Glory does not rest on the proud. It dwells with the contrite, the crushed, the surrendered. Scripture is clear: "The Lord is near to the brokenhearted and saves the crushed in spirit" (Psalm 34:18). Heaven draws near when we fall apart.

God does not discard the broken. He uses them. He chooses them. Over and over again in Scripture, He bypassed the strong and found the shattered. When David sinned grievously and fell into guilt, he did not offer burnt offerings to appease God. Instead, he declared, "The sacrifices of God are a broken spirit; a broken and contrite heart, O God, You will not despise" (Psalm 51:17). God is attracted to brokenness not because He delights in pain, but because it makes room for His presence.

The vessels that carry glory are not those that have never been cracked. They are the ones who allowed God to break them open and pour Himself in. Jacob limped for the rest of his life after wrestling with God. That limp was not weakness—it was proof of encounter. He had been broken, and in that breaking, he received a new name, a new identity, and a deeper weight of glory.

There is a difference between being damaged by life and being broken before God. Damage leaves us bitter, defensive, and guarded. But holy brokenness makes us tender, yielded, and open. When God breaks us, He breaks the parts that hinder His flow—pride, selfishness, ambition, anger, idolatry. The pain is real, but it is redemptive. The wound becomes a well. The crushing releases the fragrance.

The alabaster jar had to be broken before the fragrance could fill the room. That moment, when the woman poured it out at Jesus' feet, was not just an act of worship—it was prophetic. She broke what was precious, and in doing so, honored the One who was most precious. Jesus said her act would be remembered wherever the gospel was preached (Mark 14:9). Glory lingers where hearts are willing to be shattered in devotion.

In Gethsemane, Jesus Himself embraced brokenness. He wept. He sweat drops of blood. He cried out to the Father. And then He surrendered: "Not My will, but Yours be done" (Luke 22:42). The Son of God, perfect and sinless, chose the road of suffering so that glory could be released. The resurrection was only possible because of the cross. And the cross was only possible because of Gethsemane. Glory does not skip the garden.

Many want resurrection power, but few are willing to die. Yet Paul wrote, "I die daily" (1 Corinthians 15:31). This daily death is not morbid—it is iberating. It is the death of ego, the death of control, the death of self. And in that death, the Spirit lives. It is only when we are emptied of ourselves that we can be filled with Him. Brokenness is not the end. It is the beginning of becoming a vessel of glory.

God's greatest treasures are often hidden in broken people. Moses was broken by failure and isolation before leading a nation. Hannah wept in bitterness of soul before birthing a prophet. Peter was shattered by denial before preaching Pentecost. Paul was blinded, humbled, beaten, and imprisoned, yet wrote letters that still set hearts on fire. None of them were perfect. But all of them were broken. And through their brokenness, glory was made visible.

The problem today is that we resist brokenness. We numb it, avoid it, hide it. We equate wholeness with strength, and brokenness with shame. But God sees differently. In His kingdom, the broken are blessed. "Blessed are the poor in spirit, for theirs is the kingdom of heaven" (Matthew 5:3). To be poor in spirit is to know your need. To have nothing in yourself, and everything in Him. That is the posture of glory.

There is a mystery in how God uses our suffering. He does not cause every wound, but He never wastes one. He takes the things that should have destroyed us and turns them into altars. What was once a place of shame becomes a place of glory. What once caused tears becomes a testimony. The very area where you were crushed becomes the place He pours out His presence.

This is not just theology—it is reality. In the early 1900s, Amy Carmichael, a missionary in India, suffered lifelong health issues that confined her to her bed for many years. She had been a powerful speaker and leader. But in her pain, she wrote poems and letters that have inspired millions. Her suffering did not end her ministry—it deepened it. The glory she carried reached further because of her brokenness.

When we embrace brokenness, we become safe places for others to break too. We no longer minister from a pedestal— we minister from the ground. We speak with tenderness, we listen with patience, we weep with those who weep. Brokenness enlarges the heart. It removes the sharp edges. It softens the voice. And it makes space for God to work through us, not just around us.

The Church needs more people who are not just gifted, but broken. Who are not just articulate, but surrendered. Who are not just polished, but real. Who are not trying to be strong, but are unashamed of weakness. Because glory rests on weakness. "My power is made perfect in weakness," God told Paul (2 Corinthians 12:9). Paul's response? "Therefore I will boast all the more gladly about my weaknesses, so that Christ's power may rest on me." Rest—glory's language. Power resting on weakness. That is the mystery of brokenness.

When God breaks us, it is never to destroy us. It is always to remake us. Like clay in the hands of the potter, He reshapes us. The cracks become part of the design. The flaws become the frame for His light. And those who see us will not marvel at our strength. They will see His glory shining through.

If you are walking through brokenness now, know this: you are not being buried—you are being planted. And what is planted must break before it bears fruit. Stay in the soil. Stay under the pressure. Let the breaking do its work. Because what will come forth is not just survival—it is glory.

Brokenness is not the opposite of glory. It is the doorway to it. The cross and the crown are not rivals—they are companions. And those who carry glory in this generation will be those who did not run from the crushing, but embraced it. They will have no need to promote themselves. Their presence will carry a weight. A fragrance. A stillness. Because they have been with God in the garden. And they came out broken—and burning.

Chapter 17: The Fire That Purifies, Not Just Excites

There is a fire from God that stirs a crowd, but there is also a fire that silences one. There is a fire that causes people to shout, and there is a fire that causes them to weep. The fire of God does not always arrive to impress—it arrives to transform. Many chase the heat that excites but avoid the flame that refines. But those who carry the weight of God's presence know the difference. They do not merely seek the fire that brings visible manifestations. They welcome the fire that cleanses, that strips, that sanctifies. Because the fire that purifies is the only fire that sustains glory.

When Isaiah saw the Lord high and lifted up, the first thing he noticed was not music or miracles. It was holiness. He cried out, "Woe is me! For I am undone!" (Isaiah 6:5). That is the cry of someone who has encountered the purifying fire. Before Isaiah could be sent, he had to be purged. One of the seraphim flew to him with a live coal and touched his lips. The burning preceded the commissioning. The fire did not just light him—it cleansed him.

Purification is a word we do not often hear in modern Christianity. But throughout Scripture, it is the preparation for glory. In Malachi 3, the Lord is described as a refiner's fire and a launderer's soap. He will sit as a refiner and purifier of silver, and He will purify the sons of Levi that they may offer righteous sacrifices. God is not looking for flashy ministries. He is looking for clean altars. And clean altars are only formed through fire.

The day of Pentecost is remembered for power. Tongues of fire rested upon each of them, and they spoke in other languages. But what is often overlooked is the ten days they spent waiting in the upper room. Ten days of seeking, stripping, confessing, repenting. The fire came after the surrender. And when it came, it did not just excite the room— it set them apart. Peter, who had once denied Jesus, stood up in boldness. Thomas, who had doubted, carried the gospel to India. That was not the fire of performance—it was the fire of purification.

John the Baptist said, "I baptize you with water for repentance. But after me comes One who is more powerful than I... He will baptize you with the Holy Spirit and fire" (Matthew 3:11). This fire is not optional. It is not symbolic. It is real. And it does not leave things the way it finds them. When the fire of God falls on a person, a church, or a generation, it will burn away what cannot stay. It will consume what is flesh and leave only what is Spirit.

The Church in the West has often become comfortable with a God who entertains but does not examine. But God's presence is holy. His fire reveals motives. It exposes compromise. It makes comfortable Christianity impossible. That is why true revival is always marked by deep repentance. Not just emotional response, but cleansing. A returning. A reverence. Because when the purifying fire falls, no one walks away the same.

In the mid-20th century, Duncan Campbell led the Hebrides Revival in Scotland. Reports tell of towns that shut down because of the conviction of the Holy Spirit. People wept in the streets, not from guilt, but from a sudden awareness of the holiness of God. Services lasted through the night, but it was not because of loud music or elaborate sermons. It was because God came with fire. People fell to their knees, confessing sins they had hidden for years. It was raw. It was deep. And it was holy.

There is something about the fire of God that silences pride. When it burns, titles do not matter. Platforms do not matter. All that remains is whether the vessel is clean. The priests of the Old Testament had to go through a process of consecration before they could minister in the tabernacle. They washed. They changed garments. They were anointed. Why? Because the presence of God was not casual. The same glory that brought victory could also bring death if mishandled. Nadab and Abihu learned this the hard way when they offered unauthorized fire, and the fire of the Lord consumed them (Leviticus 10:1–2).

We cannot expect to carry the glory of God while ignoring the discipline of God. Purity and power are not enemies—they are partners. The fire that thrills must also be the fire that kills—killing flesh, killing ego, killing anything that competes with God's presence. If we want to be glory carriers, we must invite the flame that purifies.

This fire also brings alignment. It straightens what is crooked. It brings hearts back to their first love. It reignites the dimming flame of consecration. Many start their walk with God ablaze, but over time, the fire becomes familiar. It becomes a concept instead of an experience. But when the purifying fire returns, so does hunger. So does holiness. So does humility.

In 1907, a great revival broke out in Pyongyang, Korea. What began as a small prayer meeting turned into a national movement. The meetings were characterized not by shouting, but by groaning. Pastors publicly confessed hidden sins. Believers reconciled with one another. It was not orchestrated—it was Spirit-led. The fire fell, and it did not flatter. It purified. And through that fire, Korea was transformed.

Even in our personal lives, the fire that purifies is essential. It is not always dramatic. Sometimes it looks like conviction in prayer. Sometimes it feels like a holy discomfort during a sermon. Sometimes it is the Spirit waking you up at night to deal with something hidden. These are not attacks—they are invitations. The fire is calling. Not to destroy, but to cleanse.

The prophet Zechariah recorded God's words: "I will bring the third part through the fire, and refine them as silver is refined" (Zechariah 13:9). Silver is purified by being placed in the fire until the dross rises to the surface. The refiner removes the dross again and again until he can see his reflection. That is what God does with us. He places us in situations that reveal what is still unclean. Not to shame us, but to sanctify us. He wants to see His image clearly.

This process is not pleasant. It is not quick. But it is necessary. And it is proof that God is near. If you are walking through fire, do not run. Do not resist. Ask what it is revealing. Let the Spirit do the work. Because on the other side of that fire is a vessel prepared for glory.

Paul reminded Timothy that in a great house, there are many vessels—some of gold and silver, some of wood and clay. But if anyone cleanses himself from what is dishonorable, he will be a vessel for honorable use, set apart as holy, useful to the Master (2 Timothy 2:20–21). God is not looking for polished vessels. He is looking for pure ones. And purity is impossible without fire.

Jesus, in Revelation 3, rebuked the lukewarm church of Laodicea. He said, "I counsel you to buy from Me gold refined by fire" (Revelation 3:18). There is a cost to this gold. It cannot be bought with comfort. It cannot be attained through convenience. It must be refined. And that refining happens in the fire of God's presence.

We need this fire again. Not just in our churches, but in our homes. Not just in our pulpits, but in our hearts. A fire that causes us to turn off distractions. To repent of compromise. To live clean, speak truth, walk humbly. A fire that makes us weep over sin—not just in the world, but in ourselves. A fire that produces people who tremble at His Word.

When that fire falls, it does more than heal bodies. It heals motives. It burns away jealousy, comparison, immorality, rebellion. It causes us to long for righteousness more than results. To seek presence over performance. It makes holiness beautiful again. And in that beauty, God is revealed.

Glory does not fall on the altar until the sacrifice is right. Elijah rebuilt the altar before the fire came. He repaired what was broken. He laid the wood in order. He poured water to remove any doubt. And then, when the sacrifice was ready, the fire fell from heaven and consumed it (1 Kings 18:36–38). The fire comes when the altar is prepared. The altar of your life, your heart, your habits. Prepare it. The fire is coming.

And when it comes, let it do its full work. Do not tame it. Do not rush it. Let it burn until there is nothing left but Christ. Because the fire that purifies is not a threat—it is a gift. It makes room for God to dwell fully. It turns vessels into flames. It prepares the way for the Lord.

Let the fire fall.

Chapter 18: Giving That Costs, Glory That Rests

True giving is not measured by the amount, but by the sacrifice. It is not the sum in the hand that moves heaven, but the surrender of the heart. In every generation, God looks for givers—not just of money, but of lives, of time, of resources, of affection. Not givers who offer what is convenient, but those who lay down what is costly. Because the glory of God does not rest on empty gestures. It rests on altars of sacrifice.

Jesus once sat near the temple treasury, watching people bring their offerings. The wealthy gave out of abundance, drawing attention as they dropped in large sums. But a widow approached quietly and gave two small coins. It seemed insignificant, invisible even. But Jesus noticed. He said she had given more than all the others, because they gave from surplus, while she gave all she had (Mark 12:41–44). That is the kind of giving that touches glory. It is not about the weight of the coins—it is about the weight of the cost.

God has never asked for what we do not have. But He always asks for what we do not want to let go of. Abraham had many servants, livestock, and possessions. But none of that was the test. The test came when God asked for Isaac—the son of promise. The one he had waited for, the one he had prayed for. And without hesitation, Abraham rose early in the morning and made the journey to the mountain (Genesis 22:1–3). He did not delay. He did not bargain. He obeyed. And on that mountain, he laid Isaac on the altar. But before the knife could fall, God stopped him. He had seen the heart. And then something powerful happened: Abraham named that place Jehovah Jireh—the Lord will provide. Glory met sacrifice.

There is something about costly giving that triggers divine provision. It is not manipulation—it is alignment. When we let go of what we treasure, we create space for God to entrust us with what He treasures. The early Church in Acts was marked by radical generosity. Believers sold possessions, laid proceeds at the apostles' feet, and made sure no one was in need (Acts 4:32–35). There was great grace on them all. That grace—God's divine empowerment—did not just fall in prayer meetings. It rested where sacrifice was made.

David understood this principle deeply. When a plague struck Israel and the prophet Gad instructed David to build an altar on the threshing floor of Araunah, the owner offered it to him for free. But David refused. He said, "I will not offer burnt offerings to the Lord my God that cost me nothing" (2 Samuel 24:24). He paid the full price. And after the offering, the plague ceased. His costly gift became the turning point. It became the place where mercy triumphed. That same place would later become the site of Solomon's temple, where the glory of God would descend in such weight that the priests could not stand.

God honors sacrificial giving because it reflects His heart. He gave heaven's most precious treasure—His Son. He did not spare Him. He did not hold back. Romans 8:32 says, "He who did not spare His own Son but gave Him up for us all, how will He not also... graciously give us all things?" Divine giving is always extravagant, always purposeful, always full of love. And when we give in the same spirit, we become vessels through which His glory flows.

This is not about trying to buy God's favor. It is about walking in the nature of God. Givers reflect God because God is the greatest Giver. John 3:16 begins, "For God so loved the world that He gave..." Love always expresses itself in giving. And when we give out of love, not out of duty or pride, we enter into something sacred. The offering becomes worship. The gift becomes a fragrance. And God responds.

In Luke 7, a woman known as a sinner entered the house where Jesus was dining. She brought an alabaster jar of expensive perfume and poured it on His feet, wiping them with her hair. The onlookers were offended. But Jesus defended her. He said her act of love would be remembered wherever the gospel was preached. Her giving was extravagant. Undignified. Lavish. But it was pure. And in her brokenness and surrender, she hosted the glory of the Lord.

Costly giving is not limited to financial resources. Sometimes, the most sacrificial offering is time—time to intercede, time to serve, time to disciple others without applause. Sometimes, it is energy—pressing into worship when your body is exhausted. Sometimes, it is reputation—standing for truth when it would be easier to blend in. Sometimes, it is comfort—choosing obedience over ease. Whatever the form, true giving always comes with a price.

The missionary Jim Elliot once wrote, "He is no fool who gives what he cannot keep to gain what he cannot lose." That statement has echoed through generations because it captures the paradox of the kingdom. To receive, we must release. To gain, we must lose. To carry glory, we must let go of our grip on the temporal. And in doing so, we are filled with what is eternal.

In 2 Corinthians 8, Paul commended the Macedonian believers for their generosity. They gave even in the midst of affliction and poverty. They gave beyond their means, begging earnestly for the favor of participating in the relief of the saints. Their giving was not coerced. It was joyful. And it became a model of grace-fueled sacrifice. Paul used their example to call others higher—not to guilt them, but to awaken them to the beauty of giving that costs.

It is not wrong to be blessed. In fact, Scripture teaches that God delights in the prosperity of His servants (Psalm 35:27). But when blessings become excuses for withholding instead of opportunities for giving, the flow of glory is hindered. The Dead Sea is lifeless because it only receives and never gives. But the Sea of Galilee, which both receives and gives, teems with life. Glory flows through vessels that are not reservoirs, but rivers.

Church history is filled with men and women whose giving changed the course of nations. In the early 1800s, George Müller ran orphanages in England solely through faith and prayer. He never asked for money, but he gave his life. He prayed, trusted, and served. And through his surrender, thousands of children were fed, clothed, and discipled. His story is not one of wealth, but of sacrifice. And the glory of God marked his work.

God does not overlook giving done in secret. Jesus taught that when we give, we should not announce it with trumpets like the hypocrites, but do it quietly. And the Father who sees in secret will reward openly (Matthew 6:2–4). That reward is not always material. Sometimes it is peace. Sometimes it is joy. Sometimes it s open doors, divine favor, or deeper intimacy with the Spirit. But always, it is more of Him.

If we desire to carry God's presence and power in everyday life, we must learn to live open-handed. Not just in moments of emotion, but in rhythms of obedience. Giving becomes a lifestyle. Sacrifice becomes a song. And the more we give, the more He entrusts to us—not because we have earned it, but because we have proven we will not hoard it.

One of the most powerful examples of glory resting on sacrifice comes from Solomon's temple. On the day of dedication, Solomon offered 22,000 oxen and 120,000 sheep. It was an offering so vast that it could not all be handled on the altar. But he gave without holding back. And in response, the fire of God fell from heaven, consuming the offering, and the glory of the Lord filled the house (2 Chronicles 7:1–3). The priests could not stand to minister because the weight of His presence was overwhelming. Sacrifice created a dwelling place for glory.

In today's culture, we are taught to accumulate. To protect. To store up. But in the kingdom, we are taught to sow. To release. To trust. Jesus said, "Give, and it will be given to you... For with the measure you use, it will be measured back to you" (Luke 6:38). Giving is not loss. It is investment in the eternal. And nothing given to God ever returns void.

The glory that rests is the reward of the one who gives when it hurts, who sows when it costs, who lays down the best because He is worthy. It is not earned—it is entrusted. God looks for hearts that say yes before knowing the cost. And when He finds them, He fills them with Himself.

So give—not to be seen, not to be blessed, but because He is worthy. Give when it is costly. Give when it is quiet. Give until there is nothing left between you and the fullness of His presence. Because when you give what you cannot afford to lose, you receive what you cannot imagine holding.

That is where glory rests.

Chapter 19: The Secret Power of Prayer That Lingers

Prayer is not a ritual to fulfill. It is a realm to enter. It is the invisible corridor through which heaven touches earth, and earth responds to heaven. Prayer is not just about saying words. It is about releasing weight. It is where burdens are transferred, where hearts are aligned, and where the presence of God settles in a tangible way. Some pray for a moment. Others pray until something changes. But those who carry glory are the ones who do not rush out of prayer. They linger.

There is a kind of prayer that stirs emotion, but there is another kind that shifts atmospheres. The difference is not eloquence, volume, or vocabulary. The difference is presence. When someone lingers in the presence of God long enough, they begin to carry that presence with them. It rests on their words, their actions, their very shadow. That kind of prayer cannot be microwaved. It must be cultivated.

In Exodus 33, Moses would go into the tent of meeting to speak with God, and Scripture says the Lord spoke to him "face to face, as one speaks to a friend" (Exodus 33:11). Afterward, Moses would return to the camp, but Joshua, his young assistant, would remain in the tent. Joshua lingered. He stayed in the atmosphere that had just been charged by divine conversation. And in time, he would become the next leader of Israel. It was not charisma that qualified him—it was proximity.

God responds to those who wait. Isaiah wrote, "They that wait upon the Lord shall renew their strength" (Isaiah 40:31). Waiting in prayer is not wasting time. It is exchanging weakness for strength, anxiety for peace, confusion for clarity. The one who waits is the one who is refueled. And it is in that waiting that God often speaks—not always audibly, but deeply. Prayer that lingers creates space for divine whispers.

Elijah learned this on the mountain. He had just come from calling down fire, confronting idolatry, and fleeing from Jezebel. But in the cave, the Lord did not come in the wind, the earthquake, or the fire. He came in a still small voice (1 Kings 19:11–12). Had Elijah rushed, he might have missed it. But he waited. He listened. And in that stillness, glory was revealed.

Jesus, though fully God, often withdrew to lonely places to pray (Luke 5:16). He lingered in communion with the Father. Before choosing the twelve disciples, He spent the entire night in prayer (Luke 6:12). In Gethsemane, He prayed so intensely that His sweat became like drops of blood (Luke 22:44). And even on the cross, His final words were directed to the Father. Prayer was not just something Jesus did. It was the atmosphere He lived in.

Those who linger in prayer carry authority in public because they have wept in private. There is a weight that rests on a person who has travailed before the Lord. Hannah cried bitterly in the temple, pouring out her soul. She was not repeating memorized lines—she was emptying her heart (1 Samuel 1:10–15). And God answered. She bore a son who would become one of the greatest prophets in Israel's history.

The early Church was birthed in a prayer meeting. Acts 1 shows the disciples gathered with one accord in an upper room, praying persistently. They did not know when the promise would arrive—they just knew it would. So they waited. They lingered. And when the day of Pentecost had fully come, the Spirit descended like fire (Acts 2:1–4). Glory follows those who do not leave too soon.

There is a temptation in our generation to seek efficiency over intimacy. We want quick results, fast breakthroughs, instant answers. But God often moves in the slow burn. He forms character in the waiting. He reveals secrets to those who will sit still. When Mary sat at Jesus' feet, while Martha busied herself with tasks, Jesus said Mary had chosen the better part (Luke 10:42). She had chosen to linger.

Prayer that lingers changes not just circumstances but people. Jacob wrestled with God through the night and refused to let go until he received a blessing. He left with a limp, but he also left with a new name (Genesis 32:24–30). The man who once deceived had become the man who had seen God. He was transformed, not by a sermon, but by a struggle in prayer.

In the Welsh Revival of 1904, Evan Roberts would often lead meetings that lasted for hours without a single planned sermon. Prayer dominated the atmosphere. People wept, repented, worshipped, and encountered God. Pubs closed. Crime dropped. Police officers formed choirs because they had no arrests to make. It was not orchestrated by human talent—it was sustained by a praying people. They lingered. And God rested among them.

Lingering in prayer also silences the noise of the world. In a time of distraction and overload, prayer becomes the still space where clarity returns. Jesus said, "When you pray, go into your room, close the door and pray to your Father who is unseen. Then your Father... will reward you" (Matthew 6:6). The reward is not always external. Sometimes it is internal—peace that makes no sense, wisdom that defies logic, love that melts bitterness.

There is also a dimension of spiritual warfare that is accessed only through lingering. Daniel prayed for 21 days before the angel arrived with an answer (Daniel 10:12–13). The delay was not God's indifference—it was a battle in the heavens. If Daniel had stopped at day 7 or day 14, he would not have seen the breakthrough. But he lingered. And in lingering, he prevailed.

Intercessors understand this deeply. They groan in prayer when words fail. They cry out not just for their needs, but for nations, for prodigals, for revival. Their prayers are not polished—they are birthed. And heaven hears. The Spirit Himself intercedes through us with groanings too deep for words (Romans 8:25). That kind of prayer cannot be rushed. It must be felt. It must be lived.

Jesus told a parable about a persistent widow who kept asking a judge for justice. Though the judge did not fear God or care about people, he granted her request because of her persistence (Luke 18:1–8). Jesus used that story to teach that we should always pray and not give up. Persistence is not begging—it is demonstrating faith that refuses to quit. It is the posture of those who believe God is who He says He is.

There are depths in God that are only revealed through extended fellowship. Not everything can be downloaded in a moment. Sometimes, God hides revelation behind time. Not because He is cruel, but because He is holy. He wants to see who will seek. Who will wait. Who will knock again when the door seems closed. He rewards those who diligently seek Him (Hebrews 11:6).

Lingerers in prayer also carry discernment. They are not easily swayed by trends or deceived by charisma. They have spent time with the Truth Himself. They recognize His voice. And they are not in a rush to move unless He speaks. In a noisy world, they are rare—but they are essential. They carry fire in their bones, oil in their lamps, and glory on their lives.

God is calling His people back to the secret place. Not for performance, but for presence. Not to impress, but to be impressed upon. The secret place is where tears are caught, dreams are birthed, and wounds are healed. It is where assignments are given, identities are affirmed, and burdens are lifted. And it is not found in formulas. It is found in the lingering.

If your heart has grown cold, stay in prayer until it burns again. If confusion surrounds you, stay in prayer until clarity comes. If you feel empty, stay until you are filled. Do not rush out. Do not give up. The ones who linger will be the ones who shine. They will not need to announce their anointing—it will be seen. Because when you spend time with the King, you begin to carry His fragrance.

Moses came down from the mountain, and his face shone with the glory of God (Exodus 34:29). He was unaware of it, but everyone else saw it. That is what lingering does. It marks you. It changes your countenance. It shifts your atmosphere. And that change cannot be manufactured. It must be cultivated in prayer.

So linger.

Stay longer than is comfortable. Worship until the lyrics are no longer needed. Listen until the silence speaks. Pour out your heart, then wait for His. Do not treat prayer as a checkbox. Treat it as a sanctuary. Because the glory of God is not carried by those who pass by His presence. It is carried by those who dwell there.

There is secret power in prayer that lingers. Power to heal, to deliver, to restore. Power to change nations, to resurrect dreams, to break chains. But it is not found in haste. It is found in hunger. God is not moved by volume—He is moved by faith. And lingering is faith in action. It says, "I am not leaving until I find You here."

The world does not need more noise. It needs people who have been with Jesus. People who lingered. People who waited. People who are not in a rush to leave the throne room. Those people are the ones who carry glory—not just on stages, but in kitchens, classrooms, offices, and sidewalks. Because prayer that lingers leaves residue. And where that residue rests, miracles follow.

Chapter 20: Fasting That Weakens the Flesh and Awakens the Spirit

Fasting is one of the most misunderstood and underutilized tools in the life of a believer. Yet it is a divine strategy designed not for punishment, but for power. Fasting is not about starving the body; it is about awakening the spirit. It is a holy disruption of our natural cravings to make room for supernatural clarity. In every generation, God has called His people to fast—not for religion's sake, but because the flesh must be silenced if the Spirit is to speak loudly.

The flesh is loud. It demands comfort, recognition, indulgence, and gratification. The spirit, however, is gentle. It waits patiently. But when fasting is engaged with sincerity, the volume of the flesh is turned down, and the signal of the Spirit becomes crystal clear. Jesus said, "Man shall not live by bread alone, but by every word that proceeds from the mouth of God" (Matthew 4:4). Fasting reminds us that God's word sustains more than food ever could.

Jesus Himself fasted. Before launching His public ministry, He spent forty days in the wilderness without food (Matthew 4:1–2). During that time, He was not just denying His appetite—He was confronting the enemy. When Satan tempted Him, Jesus answered with Scripture. Fasting had not weakened His resolve; it had sharpened it. Glory does not rest on those who are full of fleshly strength. It rests on those who have made room by crucifying the flesh.

Throughout Scripture, fasting was used in times of crisis, consecration, and calling. When Nineveh heard Jonah's warning of judgment, the entire city fasted, from the king to the animals. God saw their repentance and relented from destruction (Jonah 3:5–10). Their fasting was not just abstaining—it was aligning. It revealed humility, urgency, and dependence on God. And because they fasted, a city was spared.

In Esther's day, the Jews were facing extermination. Before she approached the king uninvited, Esther declared a fast: "Do not eat or drink for three days... Then I will go to the king, even though it is against the law" (Esther 4:16). Her courage was not born from boldness alone. It was fueled by fasting. The result was deliverance, not just for herself, but for her entire people. Fasting preceded favor.

In Acts 13, the early Church leaders were "worshiping the Lord and fasting" when the Holy Spirit spoke: "Set apart for Me Barnabas and Saul for the work to which I have called them." After more fasting and prayer, they laid hands on them and sent them off (Acts 13:2–3). Fasting created an atmosphere of sensitivity to God's direction. It was in fasting that divine assignments were released.

Fasting is not about earning God's attention. It is about removing the distractions that keep us from hearing His voice. When we fast, we empty ourselves of what is temporary to be filled with what is eternal. We say to our bodies, "You are not in charge." And in doing so, we break the tyranny of appetites. Not just food, but lust, pride, anger, fear—fasting weakens the grip of anything that has claimed lordship in our lives.

Isaiah 58 reveals God's heart for fasting. He rebuked the people for fasting outwardly while continuing to oppress others and live in sin. He said, "Is not this the fast that I choose: to loose the bonds of wickedness... to let the oppressed go free... to share your bread with the hungry" (Isaiah 58:6–7). True fasting does not just change our appetite; it changes our actions. It produces compassion, justice, and transformation.

When we fast properly, something shifts internally. The spirit becomes more alert. Prayer becomes more fervent. Worship becomes more tender. Scripture comes alive. There is a weight to fasting that cannot be explained until it is experienced. It is the weight of surrender. And that weight draws the weight of glory.

Church history bears witness to this. In the 1700s, John Wesley refused to ordain anyone into ministry who did not fast every Wednesday and Friday until at least 3 p.m. He believed that fasting was essential for spiritual depth. Not legalism, but devotion. Not ritual, but readiness. He understood that fasting created space for God's presence to dwell more fully.

One of the dangers in today's culture is the idolization of comfort. We want power without pain, glory without discipline. But fasting reminds us that spiritual hunger must sometimes be cultivated by denying physical satisfaction. When Jesus said, "Blessed are those who hunger and thirst for righteousness, for they shall be filled" (Matthew 5:6), He was not speaking of a casual interest. He was describing a craving that cannot be silenced by entertainment, applause, or comfort.

There is a kind of glory that only descends when the flesh has been crucified. Fasting does not manipulate God—it prepares us to receive what He already longs to give. The vessel must be empty before it can be filled. And fasting is the pathway to that emptying. It is not just an event—it is a lifestyle.

In Matthew 6, Jesus said, "When you fast..." not "If you fast." He assumed it would be part of a believer's life, alongside prayer and giving. He instructed us not to make a show of it, but to fast in secret, and the Father who sees in secret will reward openly (Matthew 6:16–18). That reward is not always public promotion—it is often personal transformation. A peace that was elusive. A healing that was long-awaited. A word that brings clarity. These are the rewards of those who fast with sincerity.

Fasting is also warfare. In Mark 9, Jesus healed a boy tormented by a spirit that the disciples could not cast out. Afterward, they asked why they had failed. Jesus replied, "This kind can come out by nothing but prayer and fasting" (Mark 9:29). Some spiritual resistance requires more than casual prayer. It demands consecration. Fasting is a weapon against entrenched darkness.

When a believer combines prayer and fasting, the heavens respond. Bondages are broken. Addictions lose their grip. Fear is replaced with boldness. Confusion gives way to revelation. The spiritual atmosphere shifts. Not because we are strong, but because we have made ourselves weak before the One who is strong.

Paul lived a life of fasting. In 2 Corinthians 11:27, he wrote of being "in fastings often." Fasting was not occasional for him—it was regular. And because of that, he walked in unparalleled revelation, boldness, and authority. He knew what it meant to bring his body under submission so that nothing would hinder the flow of God through his life (1 Corinthians 9:27).

Even medical science now acknowledges the benefits of fasting—cleansing, renewal, healing. But long before it was discovered by nutritionists, it was practiced by saints. Because the deepest cleansing fasting offers is not physical— it is spiritual. It clears the fog. It softens the heart. It reorders the soul.

Fasting is not just about skipping meals. It is about being intentional with your focus. Some fast from food. Others from media. Some from certain activities or comforts. The form may differ, but the goal is the same—to draw near to God without distraction. To say with your body what your heart is already crying: "I want You more than I want anything else."

There is an intimacy found in fasting that surprises many. God draws near to the humble. And there is no greater act of humility than emptying yourself. It is not punishment—it is preparation. Jesus said new wine cannot be poured into old wineskins (Mark 2 22). Fasting is how we shed the old wineskin. It stretches us. It softens us. It gets us ready for the fresh outpouring.

In the days to come, fasting will not be optional. For those who want to carry the weight of God's presence in a culture of compromise, fast ng will be the furnace of refinement. It will separate the casual from the consecrated. It will reveal who is hungry for Gcd—not just for His gifts, but for His face.

So fast. Not for manipulation, but for manifestation. Not to prove something to God, but to posture yourself before Him. Fast when no one se≥s. Fast when you do not feel like it. Fast with expectation. And as your flesh weakens, your spirit will rise. You will begin to hear Him more clearly, love Him more deeply, follow Him more fully.

Because fasting dces not just change your appetite. It changes your life. And when the flesh is silenced, the Spirit speaks. And when the Spirit speaks, the glory comes.

Chapter 21: Worship That Attracts His Presence,

Worship is not a genre. It is not a warm-up to a sermon or a slow song on a Sunday morning. It is the sacred language of a heart that has seen God and cannot remain silent. True worship is not performance—it is presence. And presence is where glory lives. The men and women who carry the glory of God are not just skilled in strategy or fluent in theology; they are lovers of His presence. They are worshipers first.

Scripture never says God is looking for talented singers or gifted communicators. But it does say, "The Father is seeking those who will worship Him in spirit and in truth" (John 4:23). That one statement should stop every heart. The God of the universe, who owns everything, who needs nothing, is seeking something: true worship. Not entertainment. Not manipulation. But worship birthed in sincerity, anchored in truth, and saturated with honor.

The weight of God's glory has always rested where worship is pure. In 2 Chronicles 5, when Solomon dedicated the temple, the priests and Levites played instruments and sang, "For He is good; His mercy endures forever." The cloud of God's glory filled the house, so thick that the priests could not even stand to minister. What triggered that cloud? Worship. Not negotiation. Not formula. Not demand. Just hearts lifted in honor to a holy God.

Worship that attracts His presence does not begin with the mouth—it begins with the heart. A person may sing every lyric with flawless tone and never truly worship. But another may weep in silence, and heaven leans in. Worship is measured not by volume, but by surrender. It is the posture of the heart that says, "You alone are worthy." The woman with the alabaster jar did not say a word, but her worship filled the room and moved the heart of Jesus (Luke 7:37–38).

David was called a man after God's own heart, not because he was perfect, but because he was a worshiper. Long before he became king, he sang to God in secret places while tending sheep. He danced before the Lord with all his might when the ark of the covenant returned to Jerusalem, unconcerned with appearances (2 Samuel 6:14). His life declared the priority of presence over prestige. David's throne was built on worship.

The Psalms, many of which David wrote, are not just poetic—they are prophetic. They reveal the inner life of one who understood the connection between worship and divine intimacy. "I will bless the Lord at all times; His praise shall continually be in my mouth" (Psalm 34:1). Worship is not a response to circumstance—it is a decision. A discipline. A way of life. And when cultivated, it becomes a magnet for the glory of God.

Worship also shifts the spiritual climate. In 2 Chronicles 20, when Jehoshaphat faced an overwhelming army, he did not send soldiers first—he sent worshipers. As they sang, "Give thanks to the Lord, for His love endures forever," the Lord ambushed their enemies and brought victory without a sword being lifted (2 Chronicles 20:21–22). Worship was not the response to the battle's outcome—it was the weapon that secured the outcome.

When Paul and Silas were imprisoned in Philippi, bound in chains and beaten, they could have complained. But at midnight, they began to pray and sing praises to God. Suddenly, the prison shook, doors flew open, and every chain fell off (Acts 16:25–26). Worship that is birthed in adversity becomes the gateway to deliverance. Not just for the one who sings, but for everyone within earshot.

True worship is never wasted. Even when it seems like nothing changes, heaven takes notice. In Revelation 5, John saw golden bowls full of incense, which were the prayers of the saints. Worship accumulates. It builds altars in the spirit. And at the appointed time, those altars ignite with fire. A single song sung in faith can echo for eternity.

Yet in a culture obsessed with stage lights and platform presence, the essence of worship is often lost. God is not impressed with performance. He is drawn to purity. The most anointed moments often happen in hidden places—in a bedroom, in a car, in a quiet moment when no one is watching. It is in those moments that intimacy deepens. That is where glory settles.

Worship is not just what we say. It is how we live. Romans 12:1 says, "Offer your bodies as living sacrifices, holy and pleasing to God—this is your spiritual act of worship." A worshipful life is not one of perfect notes, but of consistent obedience. Glory follows those whose lives sing long after the music stops.

In John 12, Mary of Bethany anointed Jesus' feet with costly perfume and wiped them with her hair. The fragrance filled the room. What she poured out was expensive, but what she received in return was eternal. Jesus said her act would be remembered wherever the gospel is preached. Worship that costs nothing is often worth nothing. But worship that costs everything releases a glory that never fades.

When the Church learns to worship again—not for applause or atmosphere, but for the pleasure of the King—revival will come. Not because of strategy, but because of presence. And presence rests where honor flows. The fear of the Lord is not a hindrance to worship—it is the foundation of it. Worship that attracts glory does not treat God casually. It trembles before His majesty, even as it runs into His arms.

Worship also requires alignment. In Malachi's day, God rebuked the priests for offering blemished sacrifices— animals that were blind or lame. He asked, "Would you offer that to your governor? Would he be pleased?" (Malachi 1:8). When we bring God our leftovers, we insult His worth. Worship is not convenient—it is consecrated. It is bringing our best, our first, our everything.

Some of the most powerful worshipers are those who have suffered deeply. Out of their ashes rises a song not forged in talent but in fire. Horatio Spafford wrote "It Is Well with My Soul" after losing his children at sea. That hymn still carries a weight because it was birthed in pain and anchored in trust. Worship that flows from brokenness often carries the heaviest glory.

The glory of God is not just attracted to worship—it inhabits it. Psalm 22:3 declares, "You are holy, enthroned on the praises of Israel." Praise builds a throne, and God comes to sit on it. Wherever authentic worship rises, God makes His dwelling. And when God dwells, everything changes. Fear flees. Darkness lifts. Miracles erupt. Because His presence is not passive—it is powerful.

In heaven, worship never stops. Day and night, the elders and angels cry, "Holy, holy, holy is the Lord God Almighty" (Revelation 4:8). Worship is not just for here—it is the sound of eternity. When we worship now, we join a cosmic choir. We align with the rhythm of heaven. And in that alignment, glory flows.

The enemy hates worship because he once led it. Before his fall, Lucifer was adorned with instruments, created to reflect the beauty and praise of God (Ezekiel 28:13–14). His rebellion was rooted in pride—he wanted the worship for himself. So now, he does everything he can to distract, distort, and diminish worship. Because he knows that worship releases God's presence. And when God shows up, the enemy has no chance.

To worship in spirit and truth means to worship with authenticity and alignment. Spirit without truth leads to emotionalism. Truth without spirit leads to legalism. But together, they birth communion. Worship must be both fervent and faithful. Passionate and pure. Deep and doctrinal. It is not about a song—it is about surrender.

If you want to carry God's glory, become a worshiper. Let your life sing even when your lips cannot. Let your responses honor Him. Let your posture reflect awe. And let your heart remain tender. God does not dwell in every place—but He always comes where He is welcomed.

Worship that attracts His presence is not always loud, but it is always pure. It is not always visible, but it is always real. And when it rises from a life laid down, it builds a dwelling place for God Himself. And where He dwells, there is glory.

Chapter 22: Obedience Is Better Than Sacrifice

Obedience is the sound of faith in motion. It is the evidence that a heart truly trusts the voice of God, even when the instruction defies logic or comfort. Sacrifice can be performed from a distance, but obedience always requires proximity. It demands that a person listens, yields, and moves when the Lord speaks. Glory is never divorced from obedience. Where there is yieldedness, there is presence. And where there is presence, there is power.

In the days of King Saul, Israel was at war with the Amalekites. God gave Saul a clear command: destroy everything—every man, woman, child, animal, and possession (1 Samuel 15:2–3). But Saul, moved by the opinion of the people and his own pride, spared King Agag and the best of the livestock, claiming they were to be sacrificed to the Lord. To human reasoning, that sounded noble. To God, it was rebellion. When the prophet Samuel confronted him, he delivered a line that echoes through every generation: "To obey is better than sacrifice, and to heed is better than the fat of rams" (1 Samuel 15:22).

Saul's disobedience was not just an error—it was a fracture in relationship. His offering of sacrifice was hollow because it was founded on defiance, not devotion. Sacrifice without obedience is performance. It may appear spiritual, but it is absent of glory. God is not moved by how much we give if our hearts are not aligned. The true measure of worship is not the size of the offering—it is the surrender of the will.

Abraham's life stands in direct contrast to Saul's. When God told him to leave his homeland, he left without knowing the destination (Genesis 12:1–4). When God told him to offer Isaac, he rose early the next morning and obeyed. There was no negotiation, no delay. Abraham trusted the One who called him, even when the instruction threatened everything he loved. And in his obedience, he encountered a revelation of God that would mark generations: Jehovah Jireh—the Lord who provides. The altar of obedience became the resting place of glory.

Jesus modeled obedience to perfection. He said, "I do nothing on my own authority, but speak just as the Father taught Me" (John 8:28). Even when the path led to the cross, He prayed, "Not My will, but Yours be done" (Luke 22:42). His obedience was not reluctant—it was resolute. And because He obeyed to the point of death, God exalted Him to the highest place (Philippians 2:8–9). The glory of resurrection followed the obedience of crucifixion.

Obedience often requires silence. When God instructed Joshua to march around Jericho, He told the people not to speak a word until the seventh day (Joshua 6:10). No opinions. No murmuring. Just footsteps. In that silence, something profound happened—faith grew. And on the seventh day, when they shouted, the walls fell. Their victory was not in their strength, but in their surrender. They obeyed when it did not make sense, and glory came down.

141

In 2 Kings 5, Naaman the Syrian general came to the prophet Elisha seeking healing for leprosy. Elisha sent a message instructing him to dip seven times in the Jordan River. Naaman was offended. He expected a dramatic gesture or at least a personal touch from the prophet. The Jordan was dirty. He almost walked away in pride. But his servants pleaded with him, and he humbled himself. He dipped seven times, and his flesh was restored (2 Kings 5:14). His healing came not through fanfare, but through obedience.

Obedience is not always dramatic. Sometimes it is simple, quiet, and hidden. But it always carries weight. In the New Testament, when Jesus turned water into wine, it began with a command: "Fill the jars with water." The servants obeyed, and in that obedience, a miracle unfolded (John 2:7–9). They did not understand the full picture, but they did what they were told. And the first sign of Jesus' glory was revealed.

Glory does not fall on spectators—it falls on participants. Those who hear and do. Those who say yes before knowing the cost. Those who obey not to be seen, but to be faithful. When Peter, exhausted from a night of failed fishing, obeyed Jesus' instruction to cast his net one more time, the result was overwhelming abundance (Luke 5:5–6). Obedience turned frustration into fruitfulness.

In Acts 9, Ananias received a vision to go lay hands on Saul, the persecutor of Christians. It made no sense. Saul was dangerous. But Ananias obeyed. And through his obedience, Saul became Paul—the apostle who would write much of the New Testament and carry the gospel to the Gentile world.

One man's quiet yes unleashed a tidal wave of glory across nations.

Obedience is not always convenient. It may cost friendships, opportunities, and comfort. But it is never without reward. God is not looking for perfection—He is looking for obedience. Not delayed obedience. Not partial obedience. But swift, complete surrender. When we move with Him, we move in power.

Delayed obedience is still disobedience. When God speaks, timing matters. In Exodus, when the Israelites refused to go into the Promised Land out of fear, God judged their unbelief. The next day, they decided to go up after all. But Moses warned them—it was too late. God was not with them. They went anyway and were defeated (Numbers 14:40–45). Obedience out of season is not obedience. It is presumption. Glory rests on those who obey in the moment, not those who try to catch up later.

The heart of obedience is trust. We obey because we believe God is who He says He is. That He is good. That His ways are higher. That His instructions are not burdens but invitations. When Peter stepped out of the boat at Jesus' command, he walked on water—not because of perfect faith, but because of willing obedience (Matthew 14:29). He responded to a word, and the natural laws bowed to it.

The obedience God requires is often inconvenient, but it is always transformational. In Luke 17, ten lepers cried out for healing. Jesus told them, "Go show yourselves to the priests." They were still sick. But as they went, they were cleansed

(Luke 17:14). Healing met them on the path of obedience. Not before. Not after. As they went. The glory of obedience is often in the going.

Even small acts of obedience are significant. In Matthew 21, Jesus told two disciples to go into the village and find a donkey. That donkey would carry Him into Jerusalem, fulfilling prophecy and marking the beginning of Passion Week. The disciples obeyed, and the King rode in. Sometimes what seems like a mundane assignment is part of a divine moment. The glory is in the obedience.

Disobedience, on the other hand, carries weighty consequences. When Achan disobeyed God's command and kept plunder from Jericho, his hidden sin brought defeat to Israel (Joshua 7:1–12). His disobedience did not only affect him—it affected the entire camp. Obedience is never just personal. It is communal. It is generational. What one person does in secret can release or restrict glory for many.

Obedience and intimacy are inseparable. Jesus said, "If you love Me, keep My commandments" (John 14:15). The proof of love is not emotion—it is action. Glory flows through relationship, and relationship deepens through obedience. The more we obey, the clearer His voice becomes. The more we resist, the more distant He feels. Not because He leaves us, but because our rebellion builds walls between us.

In the book of Acts, Philip obeyed the Spirit's prompting to leave a thriving revival in Samaria and go to a desert road. There, he met an Ethiopian official reading Isaiah. Philip explained the gospel, baptized him, and then was supernaturally transported to another location (Acts 8:26–40). One act of obedience led to a divine encounter and the gospel reaching another nation.

God is still looking for Philips. For Ananiases. For Marys who say, "Be it unto me according to Your word" (Luke 1:38). For Josephs who rise in the night and flee to Egypt with a child because the Lord warned him in a dream. For Noahs who build arks when there is no rain. For men and women who tremble at His word and move at His whisper.

Obedience may not always make sense to others. It may look foolish. But to God, it is worship. And worship invites glory. When we obey, we agree with heaven. We align with the heartbeat of God. And in that alignment, power is released. Not because we earned it, but because we hosted it.

The most anointed lives are not the most visible, but the most obedient. Heaven does not measure success by platforms or popularity, but by fidelity to instruction. Did you do what He said? Did you move when He spoke? Did you yield when it cost?

To carry God's glory in everyday life, obedience cannot be optional. It must become instinctive. Not from fear, but from love. Not out of pressure, but out of passion. Because He is worthy. Because He is holy. Because to know Him is to follow Him.

And when He finds a heart that trembles at His word and moves at His voice, He entrusts it with more of Himself. That is where glory rests.

Chapter 23: Carrying the Cross Daily

To manifest the glory of God, one must embrace the cross—not as a symbol of suffering alone, but as the path to divine power. There is no shortcut to resurrection life that bypasses crucifixion. The cross is not an event confined to Calvary. It is a daily invitation. Jesus was unequivocal: "If anyone would come after Me, let him deny himself and take up his cross daily and follow Me" (Luke 9:23). Daily. Not annually. Not when convenient. Every single day, the call remains.

The modern Church often exalts comfort, convenience, and self-fulfillment. But the Christ of Scripture calls us to lay down our lives. Glory does not rest on the unyielded. It rests on those who live crucified. The cross is not merely an emblem on a chain; it is a lifestyle marked by surrender, sacrifice, and the death of the old man. It means letting go of the right to be right, to be known, to be in control. It means decreasing so that Christ may increase.

Paul understood this when he wrote, "I have been crucified with Christ. It is no longer I who live, but Christ who lives in me" (Galatians 2:20). This was not metaphor. It was testimony. Paul was not exaggerating; he was explaining what happens when a man lays down his agenda, his desires, and his self-constructed identity at the foot of the cross. Glory is not attracted to ego. It rests upon the one who has died to self.

The cross is where pride goes to die. It is where entitlement is stripped, and humility is born. It is not glamorous. It is not easy. But it is beautiful. It produces a fragrance this world cannot imitate. The world applauds self-expression. Heaven honors self-denial. This does not mean becoming a doormat or suppressing healthy identity—it means yielding everything that competes with God's will. The cross crucifies the flesh and clears the way for glory to rise.

Jesus carried His own cross to Golgotha. Staggering, bleeding, mocked—He embraced the weight that would crush Him. And yet, through that weight, salvation was born. He was not a victim. He was a volunteer. He said, "No one takes My life from Me. I lay it down of My own accord" (John 10:18). This is the heart of cross-bearing—not passive suffering, but willing obedience. To carry your cross daily is to say, "Not My will, but Yours be done"—again and again.

Cross-carrying is not glamorous. It often goes unseen. It happens in moments of forgiveness when revenge would be easier. In choosing silence when slandered. In serving when no one applauds. In staying faithful when quitting would feel justified. Each choice is a nail. Each surrender, a step up Calvary's hill. And with each act of obedience, the flesh weakens and glory strengthens.

In Mark 10, James and John asked Jesus for seats of glory. One on His right and one on His left. Jesus responded not with rebuke, but with a question: "Can you drink the cup I drink or be baptized with the baptism I am baptized with?" (Mark 10:38). They were asking for honor. He was pointing to

147

suffering. The path to glory is not through entitlement but endurance. Not through grasping, but giving. To carry the cross is to embrace the cost.

The early Church lived this reality. They were not admired—they were hunted. Yet they rejoiced in suffering, because they understood the cross. When Peter and John were flogged and warned not to speak in Jesus' name, they left rejoicing that they were counted worthy to suffer shame for His sake (Acts 5:41). They knew that in carrying the cross, they were carrying Christ. And wherever Christ is carried, glory follows.

Carrying the cross daily also means embracing the slow work of sanctification. It is dying to impatience, to lust, to anger, to comparison. It is the Spirit whispering, "No, not that," and us responding, "Yes, Lord." It is not a once-for-all act, but a daily rhythm of surrender. The flesh does not die easily. But each time it is denied, the Spirit grows stronger. The cross kills what hinders glory.

There are no shortcuts to spiritual authority. Those who carry power are those who have died a thousand deaths in secret. They have said yes in the dark, in the hidden place, long before they stood in the light. Jesus said, "Whoever loses his life for My sake will find it" (Matthew 16:25). This is the paradox of the cross. The more you die, the more alive you become. The more you yield, the more you carry.

Carrying the cross also means resisting the pull of applause. It is easy to live for approval—to let affirmation fuel obedience. But the cross cuts that cord. It calls us to live for the smile of heaven, even when earth frowns. When Jesus stood before Pilate, He did not defend Himself. He was not moved by the opinions of men. He had already died to them. His life was laid down long before the nails pierced His hands.

The world will never understand the way of the cross. It will call it weakness, foolishness, defeat. But Scripture declares that the message of the cross is the power of God to those who are being saved (1 Corinthians 1:18). What looks like loss is actually victory. What looks like defeat is the doorway to dominion. Glory rests not on those who avoid the cross, but on those who embrace it.

To carry your cross daily is to renounce the right to lead your own life. It is to be crucified with Christ, to let go of the steering wheel, and to trust the One who sees beyond today. It is Abraham laying Isaac on the altar. It is Stephen forgiving his murderers as stones crushed his body. It is Jesus, bruised and broken, crying out, "Father, forgive them." These are not just stories. They are blueprints. They show us the road to glory.

There is a quiet dignity in cross-bearing. It does not always weep or wail. Sometimes it simply endures. It shows up. It keeps going. It refuses to retaliate. It serves without recognition. It loves without applause. And in that constancy, glory builds. Not the glory of men, but the glory of God—the kind that shakes chains, silences storms, and fills empty jars with new wine.

Carrying the cross is also about perspective. It is understanding that temporary pain can produce eternal power. Paul called his suffering "light and momentary troubles" that were achieving for him an eternal weight of glory (2 Corinthians 4:17). He had been beaten, shipwrecked, imprisoned, and rejected. Yet he called it "light." Not because it was easy, but because he had seen the other side. He knew the cross leads to glory.

Glory is not just seen in miracles and manifestations—it is seen in perseverance. In faith that refuses to quit. In obedience that holds fast. In a life that says, "I will carry this cross—not because it is easy, but because He is worthy." That is where the fragrance of Christ is released. That is where heaven draws near.

The Church does not need more celebrities. It needs more cross-bearers. Men and women who are unafraid to die daily. Who do not chase platforms but pursue presence. Who know that the secret to power is not charisma, but crucifixion. Who understand that before God can trust you with resurrection, He must walk you through death.

Carrying the cross daily also means dying to fear. The fear of rejection. The fear of scarcity. The fear of loss. The cross silences fear by anchoring us in love. "Perfect love casts out fear" (1 John 4:18). And that perfect love was most clearly revealed on the cross. When we carry the cross, we carry the evidence that we are already accepted, already chosen, already loved. We have nothing to prove, and nothing to protect.

This daily surrender is not just for the mature believer. It is for anyone who would follow Christ. New believers and seasoned saints alike must take up the cross. There is no alternative route. The narrow road is paved with dying. And yet, it is also paved with joy. Not fleeting happiness, but deep, indestructible joy—the kind that comes from knowing you are walking in step with the Lamb who was slain.

To carry the cross is to manifest the glory. Not because you earned it, but because you made room for it. The cross empties the vessel. It removes the idols. It clears the stage. And when all that remains is Christ, glory descends. The presence of God does not rest where flesh is exalted. It rests where Christ is enthroned.

Let every yes be a nail. Let every surrender be a beam. Let every step of obedience be a climb up the hill. And know that as you carry your cross daily, you are not walking alone. The same Spirit that raised Jesus from the dead is at work in you. And on the other side of the cross is glory.

Chapter 24: Fasting That Unlocks the Heavens

Fasting is not a hunger strike to get God's attention. It is a posture of consecration that aligns our spirit with heaven's frequency. It is one of the most powerful, yet most neglected spiritual disciplines in the life of the believer. When done with the right heart, fasting crucifies the flesh, sharpens discernment, and releases the manifest presence of God in extraordinary ways. It is not about impressing God—it is about making room for Him.

Scripture is saturated with accounts of fasting that opened divine portals and shifted destinies. In Matthew 4, Jesus fasted for forty days in the wilderness before beginning His public ministry. It was after this period of fasting that He returned in the power of the Spirit (Luke 4:14). The power did not precede the fasting—it followed it. Fasting was not an optional religious exercise for Jesus. It was the furnace where the flesh was subdued and the Spirit fully yielded.

Fasting is not simply the absence of food; it is the intentional removal of worldly appetites to deepen communion with God. It silences the cravings that compete with the voice of the Spirit. It pulls the believer out of the noise and into a place of spiritual clarity. It brings the soul into submission and reclaims the heart from compromise. Every fast, when rightly approached, is a declaration that God is more essential than bread, and His presence more satisfying than anything this world offers.

In the book of Esther, when the Jewish people were facing annihilation, Esther called a fast. No food. No water. Three days of consecration. It was through this fast that favor was released, the king's heart was moved, and a nation was preserved (Esther 4:16). The heavens responded not because of Esther's beauty or position, but because of her humility and desperation. She fasted, and divine intervention came.

Fasting is not for the proud. It is for the desperate. It is not a religious badge—it is a secret weapon. In Matthew 6, Jesus did not say "if you fast," but "when you fast." Fasting was assumed, not optional. It is the companion of prayer and giving, part of the threefold cord that binds heaven to earth. Jesus warned against public displays of fasting meant to gain applause. The real reward is not from men—it is from the Father who sees in secret.

There are levels of spiritual resistance that do not break without fasting. In Mark 9, the disciples struggled to cast a demon out of a boy. After Jesus rebuked the spirit and delivered the child, the disciples asked why they had failed. Jesus responded, "This kind can come out by nothing but prayer and fasting" (Mark 9:29). Fasting sharpens authority. It exposes unbelief. It releases breakthrough in places where prayer alone has not prevailed.

Fasting kills the flesh. The cravings, the distractions, the pride—it all rises to the surface when the body is denied. That is why so many avoid it. It is not glamorous. It reveals what still holds control. But in that exposure, there is opportunity for deliverance. The flesh cannot carry glory. It must die. Fasting accelerates that death. It loosens the grip of self and deepens dependence on God.

Daniel understood this. In Daniel 10, he entered a twenty-one-day fast—not of total abstinence, but of simple, sacrificial eating. No rich foods, no meat, no wine. Just mourning and prayer. On the twenty-first day, an angel appeared with revelation. The angel explained that he had been dispatched from the first day of Daniel's prayer, but had been resisted in the heavenly realms (Daniel 10:12–13). Fasting does not just affect the natural realm—it confronts spiritual powers. It creates momentum in the unseen.

Fasting opens the heavens because it positions the heart to hear and respond. In Acts 13, as the leaders of the church in Antioch were worshiping and fasting, the Holy Spirit spoke: "Set apart for Me Barnabas and Saul for the work to which I have called them" (Acts 13:2). Fasting was the environment that birthed apostolic commissioning. It was not a strategic planning session. It was a spiritual consecration. And from that place, Paul's missionary journeys began.

Throughout church history, revivals have often been preceded by seasons of fasting. In the 1940s, a young evangelist named William Branham fasted and prayed, seeking God's direction. During those days, a supernatural healing ministry was birthed, sparking a wave of revivals across America. Later, in the early 1990s, the leaders of the

Brownsville Assembly of God fasted and cried out for more of God. In 1995, the Spirit of God descended in a revival that lasted five years and transformed countless lives. Fasting tills the ground for divine visitation.

Yet fasting must be guarded against legalism. The power is not in the act alone but in the heart posture. Isaiah 58 rebukes those who fast without justice, humility, and repentance. God said, "Is this the kind of fast I have chosen?" He then described a fast that loosens the chains of injustice, frees the oppressed, and feeds the hungry. True fasting does not just cleanse the body—it changes the heart. It moves the believer toward righteousness, not ritual.

In the quiet hunger of a fast, the voice of God becomes louder. Not because He was not speaking before, but because the soul has become still. Fasting recalibrates. It reminds us that we are dust, that we are not sustained by food alone, but by every word that proceeds from the mouth of God (Matthew 4:4). It shatters the illusion of control and brings us face to face with our need.

Fasting also invites divine direction. In Judges 20, the Israelites fasted before going into battle to ask for the Lord's counsel. They had suffered defeat despite being on the right side of justice. But when they fasted and sought God's face, victory came. Fasting is not just about breakthrough—it is about clarity. It aligns our decisions with heaven's blueprint.

One of the most overlooked blessings of fasting is that it cultivates hunger for God. The physical hunger becomes a holy hunger. The ache in the stomach becomes a cry of the spirit. "As the deer pants for the water brooks, so pants my soul for You, O God" (Psalm 42:1). This hunger does not fade when the fast ends—it increases. Because once the soul has tasted the sweetness of deep communion, it cannot return to shallow living.

There are seasons where the Spirit invites deeper consecration through fasting. These are not meant to earn more of God but to steward what He has already given. Glory requires weight-bearing vessels. Fasting is strength training for the spirit. It is not about punishment—it is preparation. It is choosing to be set apart so that the presence of God may rest more fully.

When believers fast, they also intercede. Fasting intensifies prayer. It tears down strongholds. It loosens what has been stuck. In Joel 2, God called His people to return to Him with fasting and weeping. He promised to pour out His Spirit afterward. The outpouring was conditional. It followed repentance and fasting. There are glories we have not seen because we have not humbled ourselves enough to receive them.

Jesus warned that new wine requires new wineskins. Fasting creates the wineskin. It stretches us. It removes the old. It makes us pliable again. And in that surrender, new glory is poured out. Not because we earned it, but because we were made ready for it.

Fasting should be accompanied by expectation. Not manipulation, but anticipation. God honors hunger. He draws near to the broken and contrite. When fasting is done with faith, miracles often follow. Not always immediately. Sometimes the answer is delayed, as in Daniel's case. But heaven always takes notice when a child of God empties themselves to be filled.

In a world full of distractions and indulgence, fasting is a prophetic contradiction. It declares that man shall not live by bread alone. It confronts consumerism with consecration. It breaks addiction to pleasure and reorients desire toward the eternal. It teaches the soul to wait on the Lord and to delight in Him above all else.

Fasting also prepares the Church for greater unity. When leaders fast together, egos shrink, agendas fall away, and the Spirit begins to move unhindered. In Acts 14, Paul and Barnabas fasted and prayed as they appointed elders in every church. They understood that glory must be stewarded by holy vessels, not talented personalities. Fasting ensured that decisions were made not by preference, but by prophetic leading.

The heavens open where hunger rises. The veil thins where flesh is denied. Fasting is not for the strong—it is for the desperate. It is for those who are tired of casual Christianity and long to walk in power. It is for those who want more than emotional moments—they want abiding glory.

Let the Church rediscover this weapon. Not as an obligation, but as an invitation. Let pastors, prophets, teachers, and every believer return to the ancient path of fasting. Let families fast. Let congregations consecrate. Let nations bow low. For when the people of God humble themselves and seek His face through fasting, He answers. He restores. He reveals His glory.

Let there be a holy revival of fasting. Not as a formula, but as a flame. Not as a burden, but as a blessing. Let the altars be rebuilt with hunger. Let the prayers be soaked in consecration. And may the heavens open, not because we demanded them to, but because we made space for God to dwell.

Chapter 25: Giving That Breaks Mammon's Grip

There is a reason Jesus spoke more about money than about heaven and hell combined. Not because He was obsessed with wealth, but because He knew the heart follows treasure. Wherever your treasure is, your heart will be also. Giving is not merely about funding ministry or helping the poor—it is a spiritual act of warfare. It breaks chains. It dethrones idols. It destroys Mammon's grip.

Mammon is not money itself—it is the spirit that attaches to money, seeking worship and control. Jesus made this clear when He said, "You cannot serve both God and Mammon" (Matthew 6:24). It is not a matter of balancing the two. It is a matter of choosing one. The glory of God cannot dwell fully in a heart ruled by greed. And that is why giving is a key to manifesting the glory. It purges the soul of selfishness and makes room for divine flow.

There was a reason the early Church experienced such power and unity. It was not only because of their prayer and bold preaching. It was because of their radical generosity. Acts 4 tells us there were no needy among them because those who owned lands or houses sold them and laid the proceeds at the apostles' feet. This was not forced—it was voluntary. But it was also supernatural. Something had happened in their hearts. Mammon's grip was broken. Glory filled the place.

Giving does something in the spiritual realm that cannot be fully explained in the natural. It opens doors. It shifts atmospheres. It triggers multiplication—not only in resources, but in revelation. When a person sows sacrificially into the work of God, they do not just plant money into a ministry. They plant their heart into eternity. The hands that release become the hands that receive. Not as a transaction, but as alignment with God's economy.

There is a story in 1 Kings 17 that illustrates this beautifully. A widow in Zarephath was gathering sticks to cook her last meal before death. Famine had ravaged the land. Elijah, the prophet of God, arrived and asked her for water—and then for bread. She explained her situation. Elijah did not apologize. He said, "First make a small cake for me, and then make something for yourself and your son." It was a test. Not of generosity, but of faith. And when she obeyed, the oil and flour never ran out. Her giving unlocked supernatural provision.

That story is not about manipulation. It is about order. When God is placed first, the rest comes into alignment. The widow gave in her lack, and lack lost its power over her. Mammon promises security but delivers fear. Giving destroys that fear. It says, "God is my Source, not this paycheck, not this account, not this economy." That declaration shifts things in the heavenlies.

In Mark 12, Jesus sat opposite the temple treasury and watched how people gave. Rich people gave large amounts, but it was the poor widow who caught His eye. She dropped

160

in two small coins—everything she had. Jesus said she gave more than all the others because she gave out of her poverty. Heaven's measurement is different from man's. God does not just weigh the amount—He weighs the cost. Sacrificial giving carries a fragrance that attracts glory.

Many believers want to walk in spiritual power while remaining financially closed. They pray for open heavens but live with clenched fists. The kingdom of God does not operate like the world. In the world, giving reduces. In the kingdom, giving multiplies. Jesus said, "Give, and it will be given to you. Good measure, pressed down, shaken together, and running over" (Luke 6:38). That is not poetic language—it is divine principle. The act of giving releases a cycle of divine return, not just in money, but in joy, wisdom, open doors, and divine favor.

Giving breaks entitlement. It reminds us that nothing we have is truly ours. We are stewards, not owners. The earth is the Lord's and everything in it. When we give, we declare that truth. We push back against the lie of scarcity and proclaim the reality of abundance. We say, "I trust God more than I trust my savings. I value obedience more than security." That is where glory rests.

There is also a powerful connection between giving and worship. In Matthew 2, the wise men did not just come to see the Christ child—they came bearing gifts: gold, frankincense, and myrrh. Their giving was part of their worship. It was a response to revelation. Giving is not an afterthought in worship—it is central. When we give, we join heaven's pattern. Heaven gave its best when the Father gave the Son. Jesus gave His life. The Spirit gives gifts. God is a Giver. To manifest His glory, we must become like Him.

In 2 Corinthians 8, Paul praises the Macedonian churches for giving beyond their ability. They were in affliction and deep poverty, yet their generosity overflowed. Why? Because their hearts were surrendered. They had first given themselves to the Lord, and then to Paul by the will of God. True giving flows from consecration. It is not about how much you have. It is about how much you have surrendered.

Ananias and Sapphira, in Acts 5, pretended to give while holding back. Their story is sobering. It was not the amount they gave that was the issue—it was the deception. They wanted the appearance of generosity without the substance of it. And God exposed it. Glory does not tolerate hypocrisy. Where the presence of God increases, so does the standard. Giving that is tainted by pride or deceit invites judgment, not blessing.

Some may wonder why their walk with God feels stagnant. They fast. They pray. They worship. But their finances are off-limits. The Holy Spirit does not just dwell in our songs—He dwells in our stewardship. When we open our hands, we open our lives. And in that openness, God finds a resting place.

The early church fathers wrote extensively about giving. They understood that material generosity was directly linked to spiritual authority. A heart detached from possessions is a heart God can trust with power. Not because money is evil, but because the love of money is the root of all kinds of evil. Giving cuts that root. It sanctifies the heart. It purifies the motive.

There is a reason revival and generosity often go hand in hand. When the Spirit moves, people begin to give. Not because they are pressured, but because they are moved. In the Welsh Revival, people brought their jewelry, money, and valuables and laid them at the altar. Not as payment, but as a response to glory. Their hearts had been captured. Mammon had lost its grip.

We do not give to manipulate God. We give because He first gave. We give because it aligns us with heaven. We give because it is the way of the kingdom. Jesus said it is more blessed to give than to receive. That blessing is not always material—it is the joy of reflecting God's nature, of participating in divine generosity.

Giving also breaks curses. In Malachi 3, God rebuked Israel for robbing Him in tithes and offerings. He said they were cursed with a curse. But then He offered a solution: "Bring the full tithe into the storehouse… and see if I will not open the windows of heaven and pour out for you such blessing that there will not be room enough to receive it." Tithing was not about money—it was about trust. And trust was tied to obedience.

Some argue that tithing is Old Covenant. But the spirit of giving transcends covenants. Abraham tithed before the Law. Jesus affirmed it in the Gospels. Paul encouraged generous giving in the epistles. The tithe may be a starting point, but the goal is a life of extravagant generosity. Not under compulsion, but out of joy.

God wants His people free from financial bondage—not just debt, but the fear and control that come with it. Giving is not just a seed—it is a sword. It cuts through greed. It silences fear. It declares, "I live under a different economy." And that economy is not shaken by markets, inflation, or recession. It is upheld by the faithfulness of God.

To carry glory is to release what others would clutch. It is to live open-handed. It is to trust that what is released is never lost—it is multiplied. Jesus fed five thousand with five loaves and two fish because a boy gave his lunch. The boy did not hold back. He placed it in the hands of Jesus, and glory came upon it. Giving places the natural into the hands of the supernatural. And in those hands, nothing is ever small.

Let the Church rise again as a generous people. Let us give not because we are coerced, but because we are consumed by love. Let us break Mammon's grip and declare that God alone sits on the throne of our hearts. For where our treasure is, our heart will be also. And where our heart is wholly His, there His glory will dwell.

Chapter 26: Worship That Invites His Weight,

Worship is not merely a melody or a mood. It is not confined to songs or services. True worship is a posture—a heart bowed low before the weight of divine presence. It is the highest expression of surrender, the deepest act of love. Worship is the furnace where glory rests. It is not something we do to prepare for the main event. It is the main event. It is not emotional hype or performance. It is holy engagement with the living God.

In Scripture, worship always invited the weight of God's presence. In 2 Chronicles 5, when Solomon's temple was completed, the priests brought the Ark of the Covenant into the Most Holy Place. Then, with cymbals, harps, and voices united in praise, they lifted their sound to heaven. "For He is good; His mercy endures forever." And then it happened. A cloud filled the temple. The priests could not stand to minister because the glory of the Lord filled the house. Worship became the doorway, and glory walked in.

This was not light or fluffy. It was heavy. The Hebrew word for glory—kabod—means "weight." Not the weight of burden, but of majesty. The substance of God's presence. The tangible reality of the divine. And it came not through strategy, but through worship. This glory did not arrive because of excellence in planning. It arrived because of purity in worship.

True worship is not about performance. It is about presence. The most anointed voices can fall flat if the heart is distant. God is not impressed with talent—He is drawn to surrender. Jesus said, "The Father is seeking those who will worship Him in spirit and in truth" (John 4:23). He is not seeking singers. He is seeking worshipers. Not those who merely raise hands, but those who raise hearts. Not those who know the lyrics, but those who live the message.

In the life of David, we find a man obsessed with worship. Though a warrior and king, he was first a worshiper. He wrote songs in the wilderness, danced before the Ark, and cried out on his bed. When he brought the Ark to Jerusalem, he removed his royal robes and danced with all his might. His wife Michal despised him for it. But God honored it. Glory came not through dignity, but through devotion. David understood that worship is not about image—it is about intimacy.

God's presence is attracted to humility, and worship is its purest expression. It is the sound of the soul bowing low, the cry of dependence, the aroma of love. Worship does not begin with music—it begins with awe. It begins with the recognition that He is holy, and we are not. That He is worthy, and we are not. That He is everything, and we are nothing apart from Him.

In Isaiah 6, the prophet was caught up in a vision of God's throne. He saw seraphim crying, "Holy, holy, holy is the Lord of hosts; the whole earth is full of His glory." The doorposts shook, the temple filled with smoke, and Isaiah cried, "Woe is me!" This was worship. Not comfortable, not casual—but awe-filled. And it was in that moment of trembling reverence that the Lord commissioned him. Glory met worship, and purpose was released.

Many seek the presence of God without embracing the posture of worship. But glory only rests where there is reverence. Familiarity can become fatal when it diminishes wonder. The glory of God is not common. He is not our peer. He is not a casual acquaintance. He is holy. The angels around His throne cover their faces. The elders cast down their crowns. Every being in heaven knows what earth forgets: He is worthy of all.

Worship is warfare. In 2 Chronicles 20, when Jehoshaphat faced a vast army, he did not send soldiers first. He appointed singers. They went out before the army singing, "Give thanks to the Lord, for His mercy endures forever." And as they sang, the Lord set ambushes against the enemy. Worship confused the adversary. It ushered in supernatural victory. Because when God is exalted, enemies are scattered. When He is enthroned, opposition melts like wax.

Worship does not ignore pain—it elevates God above it. Job lost everything, yet he fell to the ground and worshiped. "The Lord gave, and the Lord has taken away. Blessed be the name of the Lord" (Job 1:21). That was not denial—it was devotion. Job did not worship because life was good. He worshiped because God is good. And that kind of worship draws heaven near.

There is a cost to true worship. In Matthew 26, a woman broke an alabaster jar of costly perfume and poured it on Jesus' feet. The disciples called it a waste. But Jesus called it beautiful. Worship that costs nothing is worth nothing. Her act filled the room with fragrance and left an eternal mark. Jesus said her story would be told wherever the gospel is preached. Not because of the perfume, but because of the heart behind it.

Worship is not limited by environment. Paul and Silas worshiped in prison, bruised and bound. They sang in the dark. And as they lifted their voices, the prison shook, doors opened, and chains fell. Worship is not dependent on surroundings—it transforms them. It does not wait for comfort—it declares His worth regardless. And glory answers that sound.

The early Church understood this. They gathered to pray, sing, break bread, and adore the Lord. In those moments, the Holy Spirit moved with power. Healings, salvations, boldness—all flowed from the place of worship. They were not singing to fill time—they were singing to fill the atmosphere with truth. Their songs were not shallow—they were declarations of devotion.

Worship refines the heart. It reveals what we truly value. If our worship is cold, it is not a musical issue—it is a heart issue. A heart on fire will find a way to worship. It will sing in sorrow, dance in difficulty, kneel in reverence. It will not wait for the perfect setlist. It will not demand the perfect mood. It will say, "You are worthy—no matter what."

Glory follows worship because worship makes space. It dethrones self. It silences complaint. It magnifies God. And when He is magnified, we see clearly. Our problems shrink. Our worries dissolve. Our hearts are softened. Our eyes are opened. Glory does not come to entertain. It comes to transform. And worship is the atmosphere where transformation happens.

There are dimensions of His presence that are unlocked only through worship. Not manufactured emotion, but authentic reverence. There are moments where the veil is pulled back, and eternity touches time. Where the room shifts. Where knees buckle. Where voices falter. Where silence becomes holy. This is not hype. It is glory. And it is drawn by worship.

Let the Church return to this. Let worship once again be sacred. Not a warm-up, but a fire. Not a performance, but a throne room. Let it be the place where we lay down pride, surrender idols, and behold the King. Let the songs rise, not just from stages, but from hearts. Let homes become altars. Let lives become incense.

Worship that invites His weight is not always loud. Sometimes it is still. Sometimes it is weeping. Sometimes it is silence. But always, it is holy. Always, it is surrendered. Always, it is pure. And in that purity, God comes. Not in part—but in power. Not in idea—but in reality.

Glory is not attracted to talent. It is attracted to truth. It is attracted to hunger. It is attracted to hearts that say, "Here I am, Lord. Take all of me." That kind of worship shifts nations.

It breaks chains. It births movements. It sets atmospheres on fire.

Worship is not for Sundays—it is for life. A life lived in worship is a life prepared for glory. Every act of obedience is worship. Every step of faith. Every word of love. Every moment surrendered. Worship is not what we do. It is who we become. And in that becoming, the glory of God finds a home.

Let us worship with fear and trembling. Let us worship with joy and dancing. Let us worship in the valley and on the mountaintop. Let our worship be costly. Let it be pure. Let it be real. For where true worship is, His glory will come. And when His glory comes, nothing remains the same.

Chapter 27: The Fear of the Lord and the Manifestation of Glory

The glory of God does not descend casually. It does not dwell where there is irreverence. It does not abide where there is no awe. Glory is weighty, and that weight demands honor. The fear of the Lord is the highway upon which His glory travels. Without it, we reduce God to a concept—safe, tame, manageable. But He is not manageable. He is not a pet we summon. He is a consuming fire.

The fear of the Lord is not terror—it is trembling reverence. It is the inward posture that says, "You are holy, and I am not. You are Creator, and I am dust. You are sovereign, and I submit." It is not fear that drives us from Him. It is fear that draws us to Him in humility. The fear of the Lord is what anchors us when power flows. It keeps us from treating the sacred as common. It makes room for glory to manifest and remain.

In Isaiah 66:2, the Lord says, "This is the one I esteem: he who is humble and contrite in spirit, and who trembles at My word." Trembling is not weakness—it is wisdom. Those who tremble at His word will never take His presence for granted. They will not play with sin. They will not dilute truth. They will not exalt themselves. They will walk carefully, honorably, and purely. And on such hearts, glory will rest.

The fear of the Lord was a distinguishing mark of the early Church. Acts 2:43 says, "Everyone was filled with awe, and many wonders and signs were done by the apostles." That awe was not hype. It was holy fear. It was the realization that God was not just visiting—they were hosting Him. They had seen what happened when people lied in His presence, like Ananias and Sapphira. They knew this was not theater—it was glory. And that fear preserved the fire.

In Proverbs 9:10, Scripture says, "The fear of the Lord is the beginning of wisdom." It is the starting point, not the ending. Without it, we are foolish. We chase blessings without reverence. We pray with no expectation. We preach without conviction. We worship with no surrender. The absence of holy fear explains much of the powerlessness in the modern Church. We want God's gifts without God's gaze. We want His blessings without His boundaries. But glory does not settle where He is not honored.

Moses understood the fear of the Lord. On the mountain, he removed his sandals because the ground was holy. In Exodus 33, when Israel sinned and God threatened to send an angel in His place, Moses pleaded, "If Your Presence does not go with us, do not bring us up from here." He knew that the promised land without God's presence was meaningless. He did not want the provision without the Person. He feared God more than he desired success. That fear brought intimacy. And that intimacy brought glory.

In Psalm 25:14, it says, "The secret of the Lord is with those who fear Him." The ones who tremble before Him are the ones He trusts with depth. They hear His voice, carry His weight, and walk in purity. The fear of the Lord does not push us away—it draws us closer. Not as casual observers, but as consecrated vessels.

When glory comes, it reveals. It exposes pride. It confronts hidden sin. It tests motives. And only the fear of the Lord can prepare us to endure that kind of exposure without retreat. It is not the loud who carry glory. It is the reverent. Those who know when to fall silent. Those who know when to bow low. Those who weep in secret before they speak in public.

Uzzah's story in 2 Samuel 6 is a warning to every generation. When the Ark was being transported improperly, and the oxen stumbled, Uzzah reached out to steady it. In that moment, God struck him down. It was not because Uzzah was evil—it was because he treated the holy as common. The Ark was not a box. It was the place where God's glory rested. And it could not be touched casually. David was terrified. He realized that hosting glory required more than good intentions. It required fear. It required order. It required obedience.

Later, David brought the Ark again—but this time according to the pattern. With reverence, with sacrifice, with worship. And the presence of God was restored to Israel. The fear of the Lord corrected what zeal had mismanaged. It realigned what emotion had mishandled. Many today are sincere in their desire for revival, but sincerity alone is not enough. Without the fear of the Lord, we will mishandle His presence.

We will merchandise it, exploit it, or contaminate it. But when holy fear returns, glory follows.

Jesus walked in perfect fear of the Lord. Hebrews 5:7 says, "He was heard because of His reverent submission." Reverent submission—those two words are key. He did not treat the Father lightly. He did not make decisions independent of Him. He did not chase fame or applause. He walked in perfect alignment, and because of that, the fullness of glory rested upon Him.

When Peter witnessed the miraculous catch of fish in Luke 5, he fell at Jesus' feet and said, "Depart from me, for I am a sinful man, O Lord!" He was overwhelmed—not just by the miracle, but by the holiness of the One before him. That response was the fear of the Lord. And Jesus did not reject him. He called him. Because the fear of the Lord creates the posture for true calling.

Revivals throughout history have been marked by the fear of the Lord. In the First Great Awakening, Jonathan Edwards preached "Sinners in the Hands of an Angry God," and people wept, trembled, and repented. Not because of manipulation, but because of conviction. Heaven had come near, and the weight was unbearable without surrender.

In the Hebrides Revival of the 1940s, the presence of God became so tangible that people walking down the street would suddenly fall on their knees under conviction. No one had laid hands on them. No one had shouted. It was the fear of the Lord. The atmosphere was thick with His presence, and people could not remain indifferent. That is what glory does. And it comes where God is feared.

To cultivate the fear of the Lord is to choose purity over popularity. It is to repent quickly. To obey fully. To listen humbly. To honor deeply. It is to live as if every word, every thought, every motive, every action is seen by the One whose eyes are like fire. Because they are. The fear of the Lord is not paralyzing—it is purifying. It keeps us from compromise. It reminds us that grace is not a license—it is an invitation to holiness.

The Church needs this fear again. Not dread, but awe. Not anxiety, but reverence. We need worship that trembles. Preaching that convicts. Leadership that kneels. We need altars stained with tears, not just filled with noise. We need glory, and glory needs fear.

Those who walk in the fear of the Lord will be entrusted with His secrets, His presence, His power. They will not have to chase platforms or promotions. His glory will rest upon them. Their lives will carry a weight. Their words will pierce. Their hands will heal. Their presence will convict. Not because of charisma, but because of consecration.

It is not enough to talk about revival. We must prepare for it. And the preparation begins with fear. Not fear of man. Not fear of failure. Fear of the Lord. A fear that says, "Lord, cleanse me before You use me. Search me before You send me. Break me before You bless me." That fear is what preserves the fire. That fear is what protects the glory.

175

Let the cry of this generation be: "Teach us the fear of the Lord." Let us tremble not in panic, but in awe. Let us repent not out of guilt, but out of love. Let us bow, not to earn favor, but because He is worthy. And in that posture, glory will come. Not once. Not briefly. But with weight. With fire. With power. And with permanence.

Chapter 28: Cultivating a Spirit of Expectation

Expectation is the breeding ground of miracles. It is the silent force that prepares the atmosphere for glory. Wherever God is expected, He reveals Himself. Wherever He is doubted, His power is restrained. This truth is echoed throughout Scripture—God responds to faith, and faith is not passive belief. It is living expectation.

Expectation is more than optimism. It is not wishful thinking or vague hopefulness. It is rooted in the character of God, built on the certainty that what He promised, He will perform. Romans 4:21 declares that Abraham was fully persuaded that God was able to do what He had promised. That persuasion gave birth to expectation. And that expectation positioned him to receive.

Too many believers pray without expecting. They worship with no anticipation. They read the Word but expect no encounter. And as a result, their spiritual lives become mechanical. Duty replaces hunger. Routine replaces revelation. Yet throughout the Gospels, the people who received from Jesus were the ones who came expecting something to happen.

The woman with the issue of blood in Mark 5 did not wait for permission. She said within herself, "If I may but touch His garment, I shall be made whole." That was expectation speaking. It was not arrogance. It was desperation coupled with faith. And when she touched Him, power left His body. Jesus stopped and said, "Who touched Me?" The disciples were confused. But He knew. Expectation pulls on heaven. It places a demand on the supernatural.

Blind Bartimaeus cried out, "Jesus, Son of David, have mercy on me!" despite the crowd's rebuke. He expected something more than pity. He expected sight. And he received it. Expectation refuses to stay silent. It will not be shut down by culture, religion, or fear. It believes that God is both able and willing. And that belief opens the heavens.

Expectation is not emotional hype. It is the alignment of the heart with the nature of God. It says, "I know who He is, and I expect Him to act in accordance with His goodness." Psalm 5:3 says, "In the morning, O Lord, You hear my voice; in the morning I lay my requests before You and wait in expectation." That waiting is not passive—it is active. It is watching, leaning in, anticipating a move of God.

Jesus marveled in two places—at great faith and at great unbelief. In Nazareth, He could do no mighty works because of their lack of faith. They saw Him as common. Familiarity killed expectation. And expectation killed the flow of power. This is a sobering reality. God can be present, but unreceived. Available, but unwelcomed. Glory does not manifest where honor is absent, and honor is rooted in expectation.

The centurion in Matthew 8 needed no spectacle. He simply said, "Speak the word only, and my servant shall be healed." That is expectation in its purest form—confidence in the power of God's word. Jesus responded with awe. "I have not found such great faith in all Israel." This Gentile soldier understood that God's authority required no theatrics. Just a word. And he received exactly what he believed for.

Expectation sets the tone for every move of God. In Acts 3, Peter and John encountered a lame man at the temple gate. The man looked at them "expecting to receive something." He thought it would be money. But what he received was greater. Peter said, "Silver and gold I do not have, but what I have I give you. In the name of Jesus Christ of Nazareth, rise up and walk." The man leapt to his feet. His expectation opened the door. And God exceeded it.

A spirit of expectation transforms how we pray, how we worship, how we serve, and how we wait. It prevents our faith from becoming cold. It keeps us leaning forward. In Luke 12:36, Jesus described servants waiting for their master "so that when he comes and knocks, they may open to him immediately." That is the posture of readiness. That is what it means to live in expectation—always ready for God to break in.

Expectation is not naive. It is not blind to pain or unaware of delays. But it chooses to believe anyway. It looks past unanswered prayers and holds fast to the One who hears. It does not deny difficulty—it declares God's dominion over it. And that declaration invites glory.

In Luke 1, Zechariah struggled with expectation. When the angel announced that he would have a son in his old age, he doubted. Though righteous and faithful, his heart had grown dull in waiting. And because of his unbelief, he was struck mute until the promise was fulfilled. God kept His word, but Zechariah's voice was silenced. Expectation not only prepares the way—it preserves the voice.

Contrast that with Mary, who also received an angelic message about a miraculous birth. She did not understand, but she responded, "Be it unto me according to your word." That was expectation. Not full comprehension, but full surrender. And she became the vessel through which the glory of God entered the world in flesh.

The difference between those two responses reveals a deeper truth: expectation flows from trust. It is not built on explanations. It is built on relationship. It says, "I do not know how, but I know who. And that is enough." That kind of faith pleases God. Hebrews 11:6 declares, "Without faith it is impossible to please God, for whoever comes to Him must believe that He exists and that He rewards those who diligently seek Him." Expectation believes in reward—not as entitlement, but as promise.

One of the most tragic stories of misplaced expectation is found in Numbers 14. The Israelites, standing at the edge of their promise, refused to enter because of fear. They expected defeat rather than deliverance. Their expectation shaped their outcome. Instead of receiving the land, they wandered for forty years. Expectation matters. It determines whether we enter or circle. Whether we receive or retreat.

Expectation is cultivated in the heart, but it manifests in behavior. A person expecting rain carries an umbrella. A person expecting a guest prepares a room. A church expecting revival prays with urgency, repents with sincerity, and worships with abandon. Expectation is not internal only—it shows up externally. It shapes preparation, posture, and priorities.

In 2 Kings 4, the Shunammite woman built a room for Elisha, the prophet. She made space before there was a promise. She perceived the presence of God in him and honored it with preparation. And because of her expectation, she received a miracle—her long-awaited son. Later, when tragedy struck and the boy died, she went back to the prophet and declared, "It is well." Even in grief, her expectation lived. And her son was raised. Expectation builds rooms where glory can rest.

Expectation must be guarded. It can be dulled by delay, crushed by disappointment, or eroded by cynicism. But it can also be revived. Psalm 27:13 says, "I remain confident of this: I will see the goodness of the Lord in the land of the living." That is not fantasy—it is faith. It is a declaration that God's goodness is not theoretical. It is tangible, visible, and accessible now. That declaration keeps the flame of expectation burning, even when the winds of life try to blow it out.

The enemy targets expectation because he knows it is powerful. If he can convince believers that nothing will change, they will stop pressing in. They will stop praying bold prayers, dreaming big dreams, and taking faith-filled risks. But when expectation is present, nothing is off-limits. Dead things can live. Closed doors can open. Dry bones can rattle. Because expectation invites the God of the impossible.

Jesus often asked those seeking miracles, "Do you believe?" He was not testing them—He was inviting them. Inviting them to come into alignment with heaven. To match their confession with their expectation. In Matthew 9:29, He touched the blind men's eyes and said, "According to your faith let it be done to you." Their expectation became the measure of their miracle.

In this hour, God is calling His people to cultivate expectation again. To pray like something will happen. To fast like breakthrough is near. To worship like heaven is in the room. To give like harvest is coming. To preach like hearts will be transformed. To live like glory is not just possible, but promised.

This cultivation requires intention. It means feeding the soul with truth, surrounding yourself with voices of faith, silencing the noise of doubt, and keeping your eyes on the character of God. It means rehearsing testimonies, meditating on promises, and resisting the urge to settle for less. Expectation says, "God is still who He said He is—and He will do what He said He would do."

Let the Church once again be a people marked by holy expectation. Let our gatherings be charged with hunger. Let our altars drip with anticipation. Let our homes echo with faith. Let every heart rise in readiness—not just for events, but for encounters. Not just for provision, but for presence. For where He is expected, He comes. And when He comes, His glory transforms everything.

Chapter 29: Dying to Self - The Forgotten Door to Glory,

Glory will not dwell in a heart that refuses to die. This truth, though sobering, is foundational to every genuine move of God. The weight of divine presence is not carried by the strong, the gifted, or the ambitious. It rests upon the crucified—those who have chosen the narrow path of dying to self. This is not a metaphor. It is a mandate. And it is the forgotten door to glory.

The self is persistent. It insists on being noticed, defended, validated, and praised. It demands comfort, control, and recognition. But the Spirit of God cannot fill what the self already occupies. Flesh and glory are incompatible. One must yield. And in the kingdom, it is the self that must die.

Jesus made this clear in Luke 9:23: "If anyone would come after Me, he must deny himself, take up his cross daily, and follow Me." This is not poetic language—it is a blueprint for glory. The cross was not a piece of jewelry. It was an instrument of death. To carry it meant one thing: you were no longer your own. You were on your way to die. And Jesus said we must carry it daily.

Paul understood this deeply. In Galatians 2:20, he declared, "I have been crucified with Christ and I no longer live, but Christ lives in me." This was not theoretical. Paul lived it. Beaten, imprisoned, shipwrecked, misunderstood, slandered—yet unwavering. Because self had died, and Christ lived through him. And that death released power. That surrender hosted glory.

The Church today often preaches about living for God, but says little about dying with Him. Yet resurrection life can only follow a crucified life. We want the empty tomb without Gethsemane. We want Pentecost without the upper room. But it does not work that way. The oil of glory is expensive. And the price is self.

Dying to self means letting go of the right to be offended. It means forgiving when wronged, blessing when cursed, and loving when rejected. It means not retaliating when misunderstood, not explaining when falsely accused, and not seeking revenge when betrayed. It is not weakness—it is crucifixion. And it releases a fragrance that no earthly strength can produce.

Jesus modeled this perfectly. In the garden, He prayed, "Not My will, but Yours be done" (Luke 22:42). He could have called legions of angels. He could have silenced His accusers. But He chose the cross. He chose to die. And because of that death, glory filled the earth. The veil was torn. The dead were raised. The Spirit was poured out. All because the Son of God chose the path of surrender.

Self will always resist the cross. It will offer alternatives— good ideas, religious activity, public platforms. But none of these produce glory. They may impress people. But only the crucified life draws heaven. God does not anoint pride. He resists the proud and gives grace to the humble (James 4:6). And true humility begins with death to self.

In John 12:24, Jesus said, "Unless a grain of wheat falls into the ground and dies, it remains alone. But if it dies, it produces much fruit." The seed must break before it can bear life. The shell of self must crack open. It is hiddenness before fruitfulness. Burial before breakthrough. Silence before sound. And those who embrace this process will carry a glory that outlives them.

Throughout history, those who carried God's power were men and women who had died to ambition, reputation, and self-preservation. Watchman Nee, a Chinese church leader, spent the last twenty years of his life in prison for his faith. He could have compromised. He could have been released. But he chose to die to comfort and live for Christ. His writings, birthed in obscurity, have since shaped millions.

Amy Carmichael refused to return to England after becoming ill on the mission field. She believed her calling was not to be popular but to be poured out. She died to convenience, to comfort, to self. And her legacy remains a burning torch of holiness and love.

These are not exceptions. They are examples. Examples of what happens when the self is laid on the altar and consumed by divine fire. And this is the invitation extended to every believer: come and d e, that you may truly live.

Dying to self is not a one-time event. It is daily. It is the quiet decision to say no when the flesh says yes. It is choosing silence over self-justification. It is fasting when you would rather feast. It is waking to pray when sleep feels deserved. It is giving when no one says thank you. It is serving when no one claps. These choices kill the flesh. And in that death, Christ is revealed.

There is no glory in a life that has not been surrendered. The Spirit cannot rest upon what has not been crucified. Many are anointed in measure, but few are trusted with weight. The weight of glory is reserved for those who no longer live for applause, fame, or comfort. They live for One. And that single-minded devotion is what attracts the manifest presence of God.

John the Baptist said it best: "He must increase, but I must decrease" (John 3:30). That is the essence of dying to self. The decrease of self is the increase of glory. The less we are seen, the more He is revealed. The more we let go, the more He takes over. And when He takes over, everything changes.

In Philippians 2, Paul describes the descent of Christ. Though equal with God, He emptied Himself. He became a servant. He humbled Himself to the point of death. Therefore, God highly exalted Him. Glory follows surrender. Honor follows humility. Resurrection follows death. This is not a formula— it is the divine order.

If we want to see God's glory in our generation, we must recover the doctrine of self-denial. Not as a harsh discipline, but as the pathway to power. Not as loss, but as gain. Jesus said, "Whoever wants to save his life will lose it, but whoever loses his life for My sake will find it" (Matthew 16:25). This paradox is at the heart of the gospel. Life through death. Glory through surrender.

In Romans 12:1, Paul urges believers to present their bodies as living sacrifices. The problem with a living sacrifice is that it wants to crawl off the altar. That is why dying to self must be intentional. It must be a choice made again and again. Not out of guilt, but out of love. Not out of fear, but out of longing—for more of Him.

Those who die to self become dangerous to the kingdom of darkness. Because they cannot be manipulated. They cannot be silenced by flattery or fear. Their joy is not circumstantial. Their peace is not negotiable. Their worship is not dependent on mood. They are dead men walking—yet fully alive in Christ. And their lives carry the aroma of heaven.

Glory rests on those who are no longer entangled with this world. Who are not chasing titles or positions. Who are not obsessed with being seen, heard, or praised. They have died to all of that. And in that death, they have found something far greater—Christ in them, the hope of glory (Colossians 1:27).

This kind of life is possible. It is not reserved for monks or missionaries. It is the normal Christian life. But it is rare because few are willing to go low. Few are willing to lose. Few are willing to die. But those who do will find that the reward is not just in the next life—it is here and now. Glory is not just coming. It is available. For the crucified. For the surrendered. For those who have learned the forgotten door.

If your heart longs for more of God, do not look for new techniques. Do not chase emotional highs. Go to the altar. Die again. Lay down pride, ambition, bitterness, entitlement. Let the fire consume what cannot carry glory. And from the ashes, a vessel will rise. Empty of self. Full of Him. And ready to reveal heaven on earth.

Chapter 30: Carriers of Glory - Living as a Vessel That Hosts God's Presence

God is not looking for golden vessels. He is not looking for silver ones either. He is looking for yielded ones. The cry of His heart is not for the talented, the charismatic, or the flawless—but for the surrendered. Those who will carry His glory are not always the most visible. They are often the most invisible. Hidden. Set apart. But deeply filled with the presence of God.

The Old Testament offers a powerful picture of this in the Ark of the Covenant. It was not made of precious stones. It was wood, overlaid with gold, housing the Word of God, a jar of manna, and Aaron's rod that budded. But it was not the materials that gave it power. It was what rested above it—the glory of God between the cherubim. The Ark was a shadow. The fulfillment is now within us. We are the vessels. The glory is no longer in a box. It is in people.

When Paul wrote to the Corinthians, he said, "We have this treasure in earthen vessels, that the excellency of the power may be of God and not of us" (2 Corinthians 4:7). Glory does not come to exalt the vessel. It comes to reveal the God within the vessel. The more fragile and humble the vessel, the clearer the glory. God will not share His glory with flesh. But He will pour His glory into those who no longer seek to be glorified.

Moses' face shone because he had been in the presence of God. He did not try to make it shine. He did not manufacture glory. He simply stayed in the cloud. And when he came out, everyone knew. That is what it means to be a carrier of glory. It is not about performance. It is about presence. It is about being with God long enough that when you leave the secret place, others encounter Him through you.

This is what distinguished the early Church. They were not scholars. Many of them were uneducated fishermen. But they had been with Jesus. And because they had been with Jesus, they carried something that could not be denied. Peter's shadow healed the sick. Paul's handkerchiefs drove out demons. These were not gimmicks. They were manifestations of glory resting upon lives wholly surrendered.

To carry glory is not just to operate in gifts. Gifts can be used without intimacy. Glory cannot. Gifts can be performed in front of crowds. Glory is cultivated in the secret place. Gifts can draw applause. Glory draws repentance. It makes knees buckle. It silences the room. It awakens holiness. Carriers of glory do not entertain. They shift atmospheres.

Carrying glory requires consecration. In 2 Timothy 2:21, Paul writes, "If a man therefore purges himself from these, he shall be a vessel unto honour, sanctified, and meet for the Master's use, prepared unto every good work." There is a price. Glory does not rest on casual Christianity. It comes upon the set-apart. The crucified. The ones who refuse compromise, who guard their eyes, their thoughts, their conversations. Not out of legalism, but out of love.

Holiness is the environment of glory. Not perfection. Holiness. A life that is wholly His. Isaiah cried, "Woe is me!" when he saw the Lord high and lifted up. That encounter with glory exposed his unclean lips, and it transformed him. He became God's voice to a nation, not because of his eloquence, but because of his surrender. Glory refines. It burns away the dross. It purifies the motive. It silences pride. And it produces a vessel fit for divine habitation.

In Ezekiel 44, the Lord rebuked the priests who had allowed foreigners to minister in His sanctuary. He said only the sons of Zadok, who had been faithful when others strayed, would be allowed to come near and minister before Him. Proximity to glory is not random. It is for those who have been faithful in private. Those who minister to Him before ministering for Him.

To live as a carrier of glory is to live differently. It is to walk into a room and bring the weight of heaven with you. It is not about being loud. It is about being full. Full of love. Full of truth. Full of purity. Full of power. Glory is not a feeling—it is a reality. And when it rests upon a person, people are changed around them.

Stephen was a man full of faith and the Holy Spirit. When he stood before the Sanhedrin, his face shone like that of an angel (Acts 6:15). He was not performing. He was hosting.

Heaven was on him. Even in persecution, glory did not depart. It increased. As he was being stoned, he saw Jesus standing at the right hand of the Father. Glory does not remove suffering. It redefines it. It gives you eyes to see beyond pain into eternity.

Carriers of glory are not addicted to applause. They are addicted to presence. They are not driven by results. They are driven by obedience. They are not obsessed with being known. They are obsessed with making Him known. And in that obsession, they become dangerous to the enemy. Because nothing can move them. They have seen too much. They have tasted of the real. And they will not settle for anything less.

There is a call in this hour—not just to do things for God, but to become a resting place for Him. To walk in such deep union with Him that your words drip with His authority, your hands release His healing, your tears carry His burden, your silence convicts hearts, and your life becomes a living epistle.

This requires brokenness. Humility. Daily surrender. It means dying to ambition, letting go of image, refusing to manipulate. It means valuing His presence above platform, His whisper above crowds, His approval above man's applause. Carriers of glory are not flashy. They are holy. They may never trend. But they will transform. Because what they carry is not of this world.

Elijah called down fire because he carried fire within. He stood before Ahab with boldness because he had stood before the Lord in secret. That is the pattern. Public power flows from private communion. The spirit of Elijah is rising again—a generation that will turn hearts, challenge compromise, and restore the altars. Not through human strength, but through the weight of glory resting on consecrated lives.

Jesus was transfigured on the mountain, and His face shone like the sun. Glory was not added to Him. It was revealed through Him. He was always full. The mountain simply exposed it. And that same Spirit now lives within every believer. But He is often hidden behind self. Behind distraction. Behind sin. The glory is there—but it longs to be manifested.

To carry glory, we must make room. We must remove what hinders. Unforgiveness. Bitterness. Pride. Lust. Greed. These things clog the vessel. They leak the anointing. They grieve the Spirit. But when they are laid down, the flow increases. The oil multiplies. The fire falls.

God is seeking resting places. Not events. Not moments. Habitations. People who do not just host Him for a service, but for a lifetime. Who do not just visit the secret place, but live there. Who do not just shout about revival, but embody it. Who become burning bushes—unconsumed, but fully ablaze.

This is possible. It is not reserved for a select few. It is the inheritance of every child of God. But it requires a choice. Will we live for comfort or for consecration? Will we be vessels of clay or vessels of glory? The world is not waiting for more clever words or catchy sermons. It is groaning for the manifestation of the sons of God (Romans 8:19). The revealed ones. The glory carriers.

Let this be the generation that says yes. Yes to hiddenness. Yes to holiness. Yes to hunger. Let there be a fresh cry—"Lord, make me a vessel. Not of reputation, but of revelation. Not of ambition, but of glory. Strip away what dulls. Burn away what dims. I do not want to be impressive. I want to be holy. I want to be filled."

When that cry rises, heaven answers. And when heaven answers, glory comes. Not for a moment—but for a dwelling. And the world will know. Not because of our words, but because of the weight we carry. Because when glory rests, it cannot be ignored.

Conclusion

The glory of God is not a concept to be admired from afar. It is not a doctrine tucked into theological shelves or a distant fire we long for but never touch. The glory of God is near. Tangible. Weighty. Real. And it was always meant to be manifested—through yielded lives, broken altars, and burning hearts. This book has not been about chasing an experience. It has been about discovering the original design of the believer—to be a carrier of the very presence and power of God in everyday life.

From the very beginning, God desired to dwell with man. In Eden, His presence walked with Adam. There was no separation, no striving, no rituals. Just union. And though sin fractured that intimacy, the longing of God never changed. Every covenant, every tabernacle, every act of redemption pointed to one great truth—God wants to dwell with His people.

But His presence is not casual. It is not common. It is holy. It is glorious. It is transformative. When the glory comes, it reveals. It heals. It restores. It purifies. And it commissions. Those who truly encounter glory do not remain the same. They are marked. Branded. Set apart. They cannot return to normal, because they have seen the face of God.

And that is the invitation for this generation—to be marked by glory, not gimmicks. To be known by presence, not platforms. To be distinguished not by talents, titles, or strategies, but by the fragrance of heaven upon our lives. The world is not dying for another church service. It is groaning for a people whose lives radiate the glory of the One they carry.

There is no formula to manifesting glory. There is only surrender. Glory does not rest where there is pride. It does not dwell where there is mixture. It cannot be manipulated or manufactured. It descends where there is hunger, humility, and holiness. Where the altar has been rebuilt. Where the heart has been broken. Where the soul has said, "I want nothing more than You."

Throughout these pages, we have journeyed through the forgotten rhythms of spiritual discipline—prayer that goes beyond words, fasting that silences the flesh, giving that dethrones greed, worship that burns with intimacy, and obedience that costs everything. These are not outdated rituals. They are the ancient paths. The sacred roads that lead to the kind of life where God is not a visitor but a resident.

We have seen that glory is not reserved for a special few. It is not locked away behind stained glass or hidden in pulpits. It is available for the mother in the kitchen, the worker in the factory, the student in the classroom, the pastor in the village, the broken and the burning alike. God is not searching for perfection. He is searching for availability. And where He finds it, He pours Himself out.

We have remembered the weight that comes with glory. It is not entertainment. It is not noise. It is the very essence of God manifesting among His people. And that weight will crush those who carry it casually. That is why holiness matters. Why purity matters. Why intimacy matters. Because the closer we get to Him, the more we must die to ourselves.

But that death is not the end. It is the doorway. The crucified life is not a punishment. It is the posture through which resurrection power flows. When self is laid down, heaven fills the space. And the world takes notice—not of us, but of Him in us. This is the paradox of glory: the more we decrease, the more He increases. The more hidden we become, the more visible He becomes through us.

The burning bush was not consumed because God was in it. That is the kind of life God is seeking—a life that can burn without being destroyed. A life that can carry fire, not for a moment, but for a lifetime. A life that can glow with glory when no one is watching. That is the miracle. Not just signs and wonders—but endurance. Not just encounters—but transformation.

We live in a time when the Church is being shaken. Structures are trembling. False identities are crumbling. And beneath the surface, God is raising up a remnant—a people of presence, a people of fire, a people of glory. They may not have impressive resumes, but they have oil. They may not be the loudest voices, but they carry weight. They may not be center stage, but they are center flame. And through them, nations will be changed.

The cry must rise again: "Lord, show us Your glory." Not because we want spectacle, but because we are desperate for substance. Not because we want excitement, but because we cannot survive another day without Him. That cry will separate the hungry from the comfortable. The consecrated from the compromised. The burning from the barren. And in response to that cry, God will come. He always does.

When Moses prayed that prayer in Exodus 33, he was not asking for more miracles. He had seen the Red Sea split, manna fall, water flow from rock. He had seen power. But power was not enough. He wanted presence. He wanted the face of God. That is the difference between a seeker and a lover. A seeker wants what God can do. A lover wants who God is.

And it was to that cry that God answered, "I will make all My goodness pass before you, and I will proclaim the name of the Lord." And Moses, hidden in the cleft of the rock, saw what no man had seen before. That is the inheritance of the desperate—revelation beyond information. Encounter beyond theology. Glory beyond imagination.

This is what the Church was meant to be—a dwelling place of glory. Not just a collection of programs or sermons, but a living, breathing habitation of God. That is why the veil was torn. Not so we could visit the presence once a week, but so we could live in it every moment. Christ in you—the hope of glory. Not around you. In you.

The presence of God is not a goosebump. It is a government. It brings peace that silences storms, authority that binds devils, and love that transforms hearts. To carry that presence is the highest honor. To host that glory is the deepest privilege. And it is not for the extraordinary. It is for the crucified. The yielded. The hungry.

There are no shortcuts. There is only the altar. Day by day. Yes by yes. Brokenness by brokenness. The vessel is formed. The oil is increased. The fire is sustained. And over time, a life is built—not of noise, but of glory. Not of hype, but of holiness. A life that does not just speak about God, but reveals Him.

As this book closes, the invitation remains open. Do not rush past it. Let it linger. Let it provoke. Let it stir a cry in you that becomes louder than comfort and deeper than emotion. Let it lead you back to the feet of Jesus, where the fire never dies and the glory never fades.

You were born for glory—not to admire it, but to carry it. Not to talk about it, but to reveal it. Not to touch it once, but to walk in it daily. You were designed to be a temple. A dwelling place. A host. A vessel. You were made to manifest the glory of God in everyday life.

So go. Not in your strength, but in His. Not with confidence in your ability, but in your availability. Become a burning bush. A walking ark. A living altar. Let your life become the place where heaven and earth meet. Let every word, every action, every moment be marked by the One you carry.

The world is waiting. The harvest is ready. The glory is near. And the Spirit is saying, "Who will go for Us? Who will carry the fire? Who will make room?" May your answer be, "Here I am, Lord. Fill me. Send me. Use me. Let me carry Your glory—until the whole earth is filled with the knowledge of the Lord as the waters cover the sea."

📖 Scripture References

Introduction

- Isaiah 6:5–7

- Malachi 3:2–3

- Matthew 3:11

- Acts 2:1–4

- Leviticus 10:1–2

- Zechariah 13:9

- 2 Timothy 2:20–21

- Revelation 3:18

- 1 Kings 18:36–38

Chapter 1

- 2 Corinthians 3:18

- Romans 8:30

- Exodus 33:18

- 1 Peter 4:14

- Isaiah 60:1–2

Chapter 2

- Colossians 1:27

- 1 Corinthians 6:19

- Romans 8:11

- John 14:17

- Ephesians 3:16–19

- 2 Corinthians 4:7

Chapter 3

- Exodus 3:2–4

- 1 Samuel 17:45–47

- 2 Samuel 6:14

- Daniel 6:10

- Acts 6:15

- Hebrews 11 32–34

Chapter 4

- Genesis 1:26–27

- Psalm 8:5

- Isaiah 43:7

- Romans 3:23

- Hebrews 2:10

Chapter 5

- Genesis 3:8

- Romans 5:12

- Isaiah 59:2

- John 1:14

- Hebrews 10:19–22

- Romans 5:17

- Revelation 21:23

Chapter 6

- Galatians 5:17

- Romans 8:8

- John 3:30

- Galatians 2:20

- Matthew 16:24

- Romans 12:1–2

- 1 Corinthians 9:27

Chapter 7

- Matthew 6:16–18

- Joel 2:12

- Isaiah 58:6

- Acts 13:2–3

- Matthew 17:21

- Luke 4:1–2

- Daniel 10:2–3

- Esther 4:16

Chapter 8

- Mark 12:41–44

- Genesis 22:1–3

- Acts 4:32–35

- 2 Samuel 24:24

- Romans 8:32

- John 3:16

- Luke 7:37–39

- 2 Corinthians 8:1–5

- Psalm 35:27

- Matthew 6:2–4

- 2 Chronicles 7:1–3

- Luke 6:38

Chapter 9

- Exodus 33:11

- Isaiah 40:31

- 1 Kings 19:11–12

- Luke 5:16

- Luke 6:12

- Luke 22:44

- 1 Samuel 1:10–15

- Acts 2:1–4

- Luke 10:42

- Genesis 32:24–30

- Matthew 6:6

- Daniel 10:12–13

- Romans 8:26

- Luke 18:1–8

- Hebrews 11:6

- Exodus 34:29

Chapter 10

- Matthew 4:1–4

- Jonah 3:5–10

- Esther 4:16

- Acts 13:2–3

- Isaiah 58:6–7

- Matthew 6:16–18

- Mark 9:29

- 2 Corinthians 11:27

- 1 Corinthians 9:27

- Matthew 5:6

- Mark 2:22

Chapter 11

- John 4:23

- 2 Chronicles 5:13–14

- Luke 7:37–38

- 2 Samuel 6:14

- Psalm 34:1

- 2 Chronicles 20:21–22

- Acts 16:25–26

- Revelation 5:8

- Romans 12:1

- John 12:3–8

- Malachi 1:8

- Psalm 22:3

- Revelation 4:8

- Ezekiel 28:13–14

Chapter 12

- 1 Samuel 15:22

- Genesis 12:1–4

- John 8:28

- Luke 22:42

- Philippians 2:8–9

- Joshua 6:1C

- 2 Kings 5:14

- John 2:7–9

- Luke 5:5–6

- Acts 9:10–17

- Numbers 14:40–45

- Matthew 14:29

- Luke 17:14

- Matthew 21:2–5

- Joshua 7:1–12

- John 14:15

- Acts 8:26–40

- Luke 1:38

Chapter 13

- Luke 9:23

- Galatians 2:20

- John 10:18

- Mark 10:38

- Acts 5:41

- Matthew 16:25

- 1 Corinthians 1:18

- 2 Corinthians 4:17

- John 8:29

- 1 John 4:18

Chapter 14

- Matthew 4:1–2

- Luke 4:14

- Esther 4:16

- Matthew 6:16–18

- Mark 9:29

- Daniel 10:12–13

- Acts 13:2

- Isaiah 58:6–12

- Matthew 4:4

- Judges 20:26

- Psalm 42:1

- Joel 2:12–28

- Acts 14:23

Chapter 15

- Matthew 6:24

- Acts 4:32–35

- 1 Kings 17:8–16

- Mark 12:41–44

- Luke 6:38

- Matthew 2:11

- 2 Corinthians 8:1–5

- Acts 5:1–11

- Malachi 3:10

- Psalm 24:1

- 1 Timothy 6:10

- John 6:9–13

- Acts 20:35

Chapter 16

- 2 Chronicles 5:13–14

- John 4:23–24

- 2 Samuel 6:14–22

- Isaiah 6:1–8

- 2 Chronicles 20:21–22

- Job 1:20–21

- Matthew 26:6–13

- Acts 16:25–26

- Acts 2:42–47

- Matthew 6:10

Chapter 17

- Isaiah 66:2

- Acts 2:43

- Proverbs 9:10

- Exodus 33:15

- Psalm 25:14

- 2 Samuel 6:6–9

- Hebrews 5:7

- Luke 5:8

- Acts 5:1–11

- Matthew 10:28

- 1 Peter 1:17–19

- Hebrews 12:28–29

Chapter 18

- Romans 4:21

- Mark 5:27–34

- Luke 18:38–43

- Psalm 5:3

- Matthew 13:58

- Matthew 8:8–10

- Acts 3:1–10

- Luke 12:36

- Luke 1:18–20

- Luke 1:38

- Hebrews 11:6

- Numbers 14:1–35

- 2 Kings 4:8–37

- Psalm 27:13

- Matthew 9:28–29

Chapter 19

- Luke 9:23

- Galatians 2:20

- Luke 22:42

- James 4:6

- John 12:24

- John 3:30

- Philippians 2:5–11

- Matthew 16:25

- Romans 12:1

- Colossians 1:27

Chapter 20

- 2 Corinthians 4:7

- Exodus 25:10–22

- Acts 6:15

- John 1:14

- Acts 5:15

- Acts 19:11–12

- 2 Timothy 2:21

- Isaiah 6:5

- Ezekiel 44:15

- Romans 8:19

- John 17:22

- Matthew 17:2

Chapter 21

- John 4:23

- 2 Chronicles 5:13–14

- Luke 7:37–38

- 2 Samuel 6:14

- Psalm 34:1

- 2 Chronicles 20:21–22

- Acts 16:25–26

- Revelation 5:8

- Romans 12:1

- John 12:3–8

- Malachi 1:8

- Psalm 22:3

- Revelation 4:8

- Ezekiel 28:13–14

Chapter 22

- 1 Samuel 15:22

- Genesis 12:1–4

- John 8:28

- Luke 22:42

- Philippians 2:8–9

- Joshua 6:10

- 2 Kings 5:14

- John 2:7–9

- Luke 5:5–6

- Acts 9:10–17

- Numbers 14:40–45

- Matthew 14:29

- Luke 17:14

- Matthew 21:2–5

- Joshua 7:1–12

- John 14:15

- Acts 8:26–40

- Luke 1:38

Chapter 23

- Luke 9:23

- Galatians 2:20

- John 10:18

- Mark 10:38

- Acts 5:41

- Matthew 16:25

- 1 Corinthians 1:18

- 2 Corinthians 4:17

- John 8:29

- 1 John 4:18

Chapter 24

- Matthew 4:1–2

- Luke 4:14

- Esther 4:16

- Matthew 6:16–18

- Mark 9:29

- Daniel 10:12–13

- Acts 13:2

- Isaiah 58:6–12

- Matthew 4:4

- Judges 20:26

- Psalm 42:1

- Joel 2:12–28

- Acts 14:23

Chapter 25

- Matthew 6:24

- Acts 4:32–35

- 1 Kings 17:8–16

- Mark 12:41–44

- Luke 6:38

- Matthew 2:11

- 2 Corinthians 8:1–5

- Acts 5:1–11

- Malachi 3:10

- Psalm 24:1

- 1 Timothy 6:10

- John 6:9–13

- Acts 20:35

Chapter 26

- 2 Chronicles 5:13–14

- John 4:23–24

- 2 Samuel 6:14–22

- Isaiah 6:1–8

- 2 Chronicles 20:21–22

- Job 1:20–21

- Matthew 26:6–13

- Acts 16:25–26

- Acts 2:42–47

- Matthew 6:10

Chapter 27

- Isaiah 66:2

- Acts 2:43

- Proverbs 9:10

- Exodus 33:15

- Psalm 25:14

- 2 Samuel 6:6–9

- Hebrews 5:7

- Luke 5:8

- Acts 5:1–11

- Matthew 10:28

- 1 Peter 1:17–19

- Hebrews 12:28–29

Chapter 28

- Romans 4:21

- Mark 5:27–34

- Luke 18:38–43

- Psalm 5:3

- Matthew 13:58

- Matthew 8:8–10

- Acts 3:1–10

- Luke 12:36

- Luke 1:18–20

- Luke 1:38

- Hebrews 11:6

- Numbers 14:1–35

- 2 Kings 4:8–37

- Psalm 27:13

- Matthew 9:28–29

Chapter 29

- Luke 9:23

- Galatians 2:20

- Luke 22:42

- James 4:6

- John 12:24

- John 3:30

- Philippians 2:5–11

- Matthew 16:25

- Romans 12:1

- Colossians 1:27

Chapter 30

- 2 Corinthians 4:7

- Exodus 25:10–22

- Acts 6:15

- John 1:14

- Acts 5:15

- Acts 19:11–12

- 2 Timothy 2:21

- Isaiah 6:5

- Ezekiel 44:15

- Romans 8:19

- John 17:22

- Matthew 17:2

Conclusion

- Genesis 3:8

- Exodus 33:18–23

- Exodus 25:22

- 2 Corinthians 4:7

- Romans 12:1

- Colossians 1:27

- Hebrews 10:19–22

- Isaiah 6:1–8

- Acts 2:1–4

- Habakkuk 2:14

📖 Additional Works Referenced

- Campbell, D. (1954). The Price and Power of Revival. Christian Literature Crusade.
- Roberts, R. (1909). The Korean Pentecost and the Sufferings Which Followed. Banner of Truth.
- Müller, G. (1860). Narratives of the Lord's Dealings with George Müller.
- Elliot, J. (1958). Through Gates of Splendor. Harper & Brothers.
- Roberts, E. (1905). Revival and Its Lessons.
- Bounds, E. M. (1920). The Necessity of Prayer.
- Wesley, J. (1765). The Journal of John Wesley.
- Ravenhill, L. (1959). Why Revival Tarries.
- Spafford, H. G. (1873). It Is Well with My Soul. Hymn.
- Tozer, A. W. (1961). Worship: The Missing Jewel. Moody Press.

Printed in Dunstable, United Kingdom